Specter's

What Not to Do

London

A Unique Travel Guide

Plan your travel with expert advice and Insider Tips: Travel
confidently, Avoid Common Mistakes, and indulge in Art, Culture,
History, Food, and nature.

Sarah Brekenridge

Table of Contents

Introduction

L ondon—the home of King Charles III, red double-decker buses, and Big Ben. A wonderful town with so much excitement and things to do, but where do you begin?

Whether you have been to London already or never been, London has something for everyone, whether you are a history buff or a royal watcher.

London is England's capital and has the country's biggest urban area. With several notable landmarks, including Buckingham Palace, Westminster Abbey, and the Tower of the Thames, it's no wonder that thousands of tourists walk its streets yearly. The question is, where do you begin when planning your trip to a large place?

Planning a trip to London, England, can feel overwhelming, but it's not impossible. You can also see the sites you want to see and keep within your budget. However, given the size of London, before we can even begin getting into the fish and chips of the book, let's get you acquainted with London.

Getting Acquainted in London

As a basic introduction, these are the areas we will be exploring in this book as you begin to plan your trip to London:

- City of London

- Central London

- North London

- East London

- South London

- West London

City of London

City of London, also known as Square Mile, is London's financial district. This is the area in which the city developed and has always been the center for trading, settlements, and ceremonies since the Roman era. In this area of London, you will find its oldest and deepest history, as it is the country's foundational part. Here you will see ruins from the Roman period, the famous Tower Bridge, and some beautiful gardens to begin to understand how London began to grow into what it is today.

Central London

Located in the innermost part of London is Central London. Several boroughs make up central London, most notably Kensington and Chelsea. Central London is the part of the country most people know of (or likely think of) because it is the country's hub. Here is where you can explore some famous neighborhoods, including Westminster and King's Cross, in addition to seeing Buckingham Palace and watching the Changing of the Guards.

North London

North London is well-known for its architecture, historical monuments, and artistic structures. This area is well-loved and respected for its cultural and historical significance. North London is one of the top areas for Harry Potter fans to explore because of its various ties to the movie sets. This part of London is also famous for Abbey Road—people love walking across the famous crosswalk, as famously photographed by The Beatles walking across it for their 1969 album, *Abbey Road.*

East London

Although East London is well-known for being the area where Jack the Ripper terrorized the community, this part of London is a cultural spot where you can immerse yourself in several activities. Every street is unique in this area, which makes it more exciting.

If Jack the Ripper is not up your alley (because it was a pretty dark time), you may enjoy East London for its Shakespearean history! Shakespeare is connected to East London, and learning more about his life as a playwright and poet with his influence in the performing and literary arts is exciting for many literary fans!

South London

South London offers some of the most gorgeous parks in the city. This region has many well-known homes, monuments, and other landmarks. However, it's also where tennis fans gather every summer in Wimbledon to watch the tennis tournament. Fans worldwide, celebrities, and the Royals will come to watch some of the sport's best players compete and battle it out on the courts for the champion title.

West London

West London is the famed wealthy region of the city. However, it's also a museum-lovers haven for its many museums, conveniently located next to one another. Additionally, West London is where you will find Paddington, the famous bear with a blue duffle coat and red hat. Her Majesty adored this bear (as do millions of kids) for his mischief. There are plenty of other areas to explore in West London, so you can guarantee you'll never run out of things to do and experience here!

London is a place that is full of adventure. It's busy. It's entertaining. It's a one-of-a-kind city. There are plenty of ways to plan your trip. But as I am a travel enthusiast, my goal is to make your trip planning seamless. In this book, we will work on planning your trip to London. We'll go through the different parts of London (more in-depth), several popular sites, things you should experience, and how to keep yourself safe in one of the largest cities. In addition, we'll discuss some of the pitfalls you should avoid as a tourist to make you not look like a tourist, among other things. At the end of this book, you will feel confident in how you want to plan your trip to London and the exciting memories you will make.

Chapter 1:

Planning Your Trip to London

W hy should everyone visit London? That is the question—especially since London is one of the most expensive cities to visit. But it is unlike any other city in the world, and more people are visiting it today—especially since the COVID-19 pandemic ended. London was one of the most visited cities in 2022. The United Kingdom's (U.K.) capital saw about 16 million people visit. It was lower than before the coronavirus hit the world by 26%, but the more people become open to traveling again, the more people want to fly to places like London (Statista Research Department, 2023).

Best Time to Go to London

There isn't a specific time of year you should or should not go to London because you can see and experience the attractions and monuments at any time. However, London's better weather typically happens during the late spring to early summer (May and June) and late summer to early autumn (September and October).

The Climate and Seasons of London

Every season in London comes with its own beauty. Knowing the seasons and expected temperatures will make packing seamless whenever you plan to go to the vibrant United Kingdom city.

If you plan to go to London during the spring (March to May) or autumn (September to November), you can expect temperatures to reach between 52°F and 64°F during the day and between 43°F and 55°F in the evenings. You will want to pack some long pants and sweaters if you plan to visit London during these two seasons to ensure you are warm enough.

If you go to London in the summer, the city has recently seen record-high temperatures above 86°F. However, outside of the heat waves, temperatures reach about 64°F during the day and about 57°F in the evening. You'll want to pack at least one or two pairs of shorts if you're going to London in the summer, but also pack some pants and a sweater.

In the winter, London sees temperatures between 35°F and 50°F. They don't typically see snow (more cold rain than anything). However, there are some fun

Christmas decorations around Christmas, and the city will display impressive fireworks on New Year's Eve!

Seasons aside, London is well-known for being a rainy city. Throughout the year, they may see about 11 to 15 rainy days each month. The rainfall is highest in August and November and lowest between March and April. Either way, pack a raincoat anyway!

Tourist Seasons

Depending on when you want to go to London, you should also be mindful of the three tourist seasons: low season, shoulder season, and high season:

Low season: London's lowest season for tourists is understandably going to be during the late autumn to late winter months (November to February). If you are okay with the weather not being the greatest, this is the best time to go to London. You'll still be able to see many of the major attractions indoors (without it being overly crowded), and your flight and accommodations will be cheaper.

Shoulder season: Shoulder season is on either side of the high seasons (between March and April and mid-September and October). You can expect the city to feel less crowded if you go during these months, and you're less likely to see as much rainfall.

High season: High season in London happens during the summer months. The summer months can be both rainy and humid, but several events during these months encourage tourists to come to London.

Best Seasons to Go to London

Now that you have a basic understanding of the climate and seasons in London, here is what you can expect based on when you go:

Springtime in London: Spring in London is between March and May. This is when London starts to smell like spring, with its flowers blooming throughout the parks and gardens. The city's vibrant colors returning to life from the dreary winter make it all the more charming as you wander the streets. (Plus, the tourist season hasn't fully hit yet, making wandering around all the more pleasant!)

Summertime in London: Summer in London is from June until August. As I said earlier, in recent years, London has seen record-high temperatures during the heat waves instead of intermittent showers. Despite the weather, summer is an excellent time to see various festivals, markets, and more.

Autumn in London: Autumn in London starts in September and lasts until about the middle of November. This season, you'll see a lovely warm tone to the foliage around the city. It's also lively, with Halloween and the holidays coming soon after.

Winter in London: Winter in London will be cold and damp. But don't let the coldness chill your spirit! Although winter in London is from mid-November until February, there are plenty of things to see and do (and the tourist crowds will be minimal). If you go here around Christmas, you'll see some beautiful Christmas lights to light up the city.

London's Year-Round Charms

London has plenty of places to experience and explore. Let's explore some year-round charms you can check out each month.

January

January is frigid! But that doesn't stop the fun in this old London town! Going to London in January is ideal to avoid crowds, especially in museums, art galleries, and other attractions. The city is still celebrating various things with the new year in place. You'll find plenty of workshops and pop-up shops around the city. January is also when the London Short Film Festival will take place, and if you're a Harry Potter fan, going to the Warner Bros. Studios to see Hogwarts in the Snow is a must!

February

London sees some unpredictable weather in February, with (what seems like) endless days of rain throughout the month. However, with the weather being adverse, damp, and cold, the tourist season is still relatively slow, allowing you to experience London in a pristine condition. However, London is quite romantic for those who love Valentine's Day and are looking for a getaway with their partner. London also has their fashion week this month. In addition, you should look for some live music and cabaret shows to check out!

March

Ah—the smell of spring is in the air in London when March comes around. London will start to shed its chilly dampness for the warmer weather. Rain is still a constant (but at least it'll help those flowers bloom). If you come to London during March, you'll see the city paint itself in vibrant colors to mark Mother's Day and St. Patrick's Day. Don't forget also to check out the Battersea Spring Affordable Art Fair!

April

April is when London will finally see some better weather. This is the time to wander around the various gardens to see the blooming flowers. If Easter is happening this month (since it sometimes occurs in March), London will have several Easter celebrations and interactive activities. If you love sporting events, the London Marathon, which attracts worldwide attention, runs (no pun intended) during this month. You should also go to the Underbelly Festival, which celebrates the performing arts.

May

Spring is in full swing during May, and still not quite a tourist season, making this month a pleasant time to be in London. A cruise along the Thames is a good choice so you can see London differently. If you're into photography or arts and crafts, the London Craft Week and the Photo London events happen this month. However, it's in May when the popular football league (the English way to say soccer and how it will be referred to in this book), the English Premier League, starts up!

June

With summer officially rolling into London during June, everything in the city seems to become alive overnight! The streets will start to see more travelers roaming around, the Taste of London Food Festival will happen, and you can check out some art and craft exhibitions.

July

London in July is a perfect month for outdoor activities and picnics. While the famous landmarks are open year-round, this is the month when the tourist season is in full swing. Be sure to pack your patience if you're going to any of the monuments and landmarks.

In addition, July is when Wimbledon will take place! Cricket season also starts in July. The Underbelly Festival will continue this month for performing arts enthusiasts, but you will also see several music festivals coming into London.

August

August is one of the best months to go to London if you plan to travel with your family, as several family-friendly events are happening. You can expect the tourist crowd to be quite busy during August, so depending on how long you'll be in London, you may want to take a day trip outside the city to places like Saltburn-by-the-Sea, Dover, or the Cotswolds.

September

As summer starts to wind down, so does the tourist season. This will make for pleasant strolls through the city and wandering through monuments without feeling like a fish in a can. In September, London celebrates the Thames River history with several exhibitions around the river. Some other attractions worth checking out include the Japan Matsuri and the London Design Festival.

October

As the leaves change colors in London, you might see the locals kicking back a little more with the tourist season dwindling. Going to Richmond Park or Kew Gardens to see the autumn colors is a must! For festivals and events, London will show some of its multicultural sides with events that celebrate Diwali and Africa.

If you enjoy cocktails, the London Cocktail Week and London Restaurant Festival will occur in October.

November

London in November is a perfect time to go if you want to avoid crazy crowds. If you want to check out some other events, London puts on the Regent Park Motor Show and the London Jazz Festival. After you are done adventuring for the day, cozy up in one of their many pubs to enjoy comfort food and cider.

December

Christmas season has arrived in London with twinkling Christmas lights to signify holiday cheer. There are several Christmas markets to check out in London. In addition, Hyde Park, Trafalgar Square, and Kew Gardens are set up for the holiday season and are worth a stroll through.

Booking Essentials for London

Careful planning and booking for attractions is a must, especially if planning to go to London beforehand. That goes for flights and accommodations, too. This section will cover all the important pieces you should consider when planning your trip. While there is no simple answer as to how far in advance you should book some of the attractions, keeping in mind the tourist seasons will help you decide which ones you really want to see. I would recommend making a list (or highlighting) of the ones you want to see in order of priority to ensure you book the tickets! But before we get to that point, let's discuss flights.

Flying to London

Given London's size, it should be no surprise that they have six major international airports.

London Heathrow Airport

London Heathrow Airport is the United Kingdom's biggest airport, serving around 80 million flyers yearly. This is one of the main hubs many fly into, as it has five terminals and serves over 80 airlines, making it seamless for people to connect to other parts of the world.

Gatwick Airport

As the second largest airport in the United Kingdom, Gatwick Airport serves over 40 million passengers yearly. This airport helps people connect to over 200 destinations worldwide.

Stansted Airport

The Stansted Airport is around 42 miles from London, serving around 28 million passengers annually. This airport has several low-cost airlines that fly into it.

Luton Airport

Luton Airport is another hub that services several low-cost flight services. If you're trying to save on flights, flying into this airport is an excellent option, and it is only 27 miles from the center of London.

London Southend Airport

London Southend Airport is the smallest airport in the United Kingdom, serving about 1.4 million passengers yearly. Like Luton and Stansted, it's a popular airport for low-cost airlines.

London City Airport

London City Airport is the closest to London's city center. It's one of the newer airports, but as it's not significantly large, it does not get overly busy. This airport also hosts air shows!

Finding the Right Flight

Do you go cheap or pay for a higher-end plane ticket when planning a trip to London? Most seasoned travelers are experienced in searching for the best flights to their destinations—for the more unseasoned travelers, booking flights can be daunting.

Flying to London requires going "over the pond," as the saying goes. It's not necessarily a short flight, but it's also understandable if you don't want to spend significant money to get you there. Thus, one of the first things you should be doing is utilizing flight search engines, such as Skyscanner, Momondo, and JetRadar.

However, I wouldn't go right ahead and use your regular browser for this. There's a reason why our computers have cookies. When we enter our data (say, the dates you're floating around to go to London), the cookies will be tracked (like breadcrumbs) and fed to the websites, and *poof!*, there goes the original flight costs and is replaced with inflated prices. Our web browsers have a nifty little secret called an incognito browser that allows you to browse privately as your cookies reset every time you enter a new private browsing window. Get into the habit of using this, as it will help you to avoid the dreaded inflated prices.

That said, if you can, be flexible on the dates you want to arrive—unless you have already booked tour guide tickets. If you have already booked tours to see attractions, you can still be creative in looking for cheap flight options. Skyscanner's search tool allows you to search prices for the month rather than just your specified travel dates. However, some helpful tips are to avoid flying over the weekends (including Fridays) as these days tend to be busier. Instead, compare the prices to flying Monday to Monday or Tuesday to Tuesday. In that search, consider looking for the cheapest airport (most flight search engines allow you to choose airports near your destination).

Lastly, if you are willing to fly to London during the off-peak season, do it! You'll find fewer crowds, and flights will be significantly cheaper.

Finding Accommodations

One thing to remember when looking for accommodations is that you must have a good, trusty base. You want a clean, safe place that puts the guests first. There are plenty of options for accommodations. You can rent VRBO homes or an Airbnb or choose to stay in hostels, bed and breakfasts, or hotels. The important thing is that no matter what option you choose, you want to do your research. Just because the price is right does not mean the hotel is by any means up to standards (and keep in mind, every country differs in standards). However, that's not to say that budget hotels should be entirely off your list. If you're sticking to a budget, it comes down to reviews and what other guests say. If several of those reviews rate the accommodation crappy, don't bother.

As London is a large city, consider your location choice. Staying in central London is ideal because it's near almost everything. If you stay further outside of London, your commute can take up some of the time you want to be adventuring through London. Some accommodations may say they're near everything, but look at the map. Are they near a tube station? How long would it take for you to get from point A to point B? These are the things to keep in mind.

Activities and Tours

In this era, booking your tickets in advance is the way to go. But should you book everything you want to see in advance, or can you buy some tickets on the day of? Booking some of the things you want to see (in other words, you would regret it if you didn't) is a great idea, but leaving some room for a day of activities is a healthy balance. Some places you should book in advance include tours of the Buckingham Palace state rooms (summer months only), tours of the Harry Potter studio, Westminster Abbey, Churchill War Rooms, SkyGarden, and tours of the Houses of Parliament.

Museums are places you can show up to and buy tickets on the day of (but you can also check to see about buying your tickets ahead of time to avoid standing in long lines).

As for other tours, there are options available that can help you efficiently see London and maximize your time in the city! Some of these tours include

London in 48 hours: This tour will take you through London with the ease of a bus you can hop on and off. There are 70 stops with four different routes, allowing you to tick off seeing many major attractions. In addition, your ticket includes a boat cruise along the Thames.

Total London Experience: This day tour is a packed tour that takes you through St. Paul's Cathedral, view the Crown Jewels at the Tower of London, see the Changing the Guard at Buckingham, and ride the London Eye.

London After Dark: This 90-minute tour takes you for a ride on an open-top bus through the Houses of Parliament, Big Ben, Trafalgar Square, the London Eyes, Buckingham Palace, and Piccadilly Circus, giving you a different perspective of what London looks like at night.

Beyond London Tours: This company offers day-trip tours which will take you to Windsor Castle and the mysterious Stonehenge.

Visa and Requirements

If you're planning a trip to the United Kingdom for tourism, visiting family and friends, or attending business meetings, you may need to obtain a Standard Visitor Visa. This visa allows you to stay in the UK for up to six months and engage in various activities during your visit. To ensure a smooth journey, it's essential to understand the visa requirements and application process:

Eligibility: The Standard Visitor Visa is generally available to citizens of countries outside the European Economic Area (EEA) and Switzerland. However, some nationalities may be exempt from obtaining a visa for short visits. It's crucial to check the UK government's official website or consult the nearest British embassy or consulate to determine your eligibility. United States of America citizens can enter and travel through the United Kingdom for up to six months without a visa. However, you must apply for a visa if you intend to stay longer than six months.

Passport Validity: For traveling to the UK, your passport must be valid for the entire duration of your stay. Ensure it's not set to expire during your trip. It's also advisable to have at least six months of validity beyond your intended departure date, as some airlines and immigration authorities may enforce this rule.

Application Process: To apply for a Standard Visitor Visa, you will typically need to complete an online application form, pay the visa fee, and book an appointment at a Visa Application Center in your home country. You may also be required to provide biometric data, such as fingerprints and a digital photograph.

Supporting Documents: You'll need to submit various documents, including a valid passport, proof of your travel itinerary (including accommodation bookings), evidence of sufficient funds to cover your stay, and a letter outlining the purpose of your visit. If you're visiting friends or family, you'll also need an invitation letter from your host.

Financial Requirements: You must demonstrate that you can financially support yourself during your stay in the UK. The exact amount required may vary, so it's essential to check the current financial thresholds.

Intentions and Ties to Your Home Country: You must provide evidence of your intentions to return to your home country after your UK visit. This may include proof of employment, property ownership, or family ties.

Packing Tips

The big question about traveling to London: How do you pack for it? A few things will determine what you need to bring, mainly the seasons. If it's spring or autumn, you'll want warmer clothes. If it's winter, you will want clothes to bundle up in; in the summer, you'll want some clothes you won't melt in. Your essential packing list should include these items:

- tank tops or basic T-shirts

- sweater or a sweatshirt
- jeans or pants
- underwear
- socks
- shoes (a comfortable pair of sneakers for walking and a nice pair)
- formal clothing (if needed)
- rain jacket
- rainproof shoes or boots
- toothpaste and toothbrush
- deodorant
- moisturizer
- sunscreen
- other hygiene products

In your carry-on, you should have your

- passport
- travel adaptor
- cellphone
- laptop or tablet
- charging cords
- medications
- books or e-reader

Cold Weather Clothing

If you're going to London in colder seasons, make sure to pack the following:

- winter coat
- gloves
- scarf hat

Another important thing you should consider purchasing before going to London is a prepaid European SIM or E-SIM phone card. Roaming charges are expensive through carriers, but by purchasing a SIM card for your phone, you'll still have data in London without the headache of extra charges. Orange Travel is a popular company for SIM cards which you can get on Amazon or their website.

Currency Exchange and Money-Saving Tips

The currency in London is the pound with this symbol: £. (Anything less than one pound is referred to as a pence). It's always best to get your currency before you leave the US. However, if you need or want more cash, currency exchange companies, such as the Bureau de Change, can assist you in places like train stations and airports. Otherwise, you can use your bank card to withdraw funds from an ATM but expect charges to occur (so it's probably better to go to a currency exchange counter instead).

As for saving money, there are plenty of ways to do so with these handy tips:

- **Travel with an Oyster Card:** Oyster Cards are contactless payment options for getting around London. The visitor Oyster Card is 50% cheaper than buying single tickets or paying with cash.

- **Walk:** Although public transportation is handy for getting around London (especially for attractions further apart), walking is ideal (especially in Central London). Plus, walking allows you to see other sights you might not have seen otherwise if you were underground on the tube.

- **Take advantage of free attractions:** London has several attractions and landmarks that don't require an admission fee. These attractions include the National Gallery, British Museum (though you will still need to book your time slot), Southbank Center, Hyde Park, and Hampstead Heath.

- **West End Theatre shows:** Book your tickets far in advance if you want to see a live West End Theater show. However, if you don't do this and you want last-minute tickets, you can buy them at the TKTS booth in Leicester Square for cheap!

- **Book online in advance:** As there are some attractions you should purchase in advance, you may be lucky and save on the ticketed attractions.

- **Cheap eats:** Unless you rent an Airbnb or VRBO home, you likely will eat out often. Look for chain restaurants or traditional cafés for affordable food. In nice weather, picking up a premade sandwich from a supermarket or shop or something from a food truck to picnic in one of London's parks, courtyards, or gardens is also a great option.

What to Avoid When Planning a Trip to London

London is a popular place for many people to travel to, and it's no surprise with its history, the Royals, and beautiful architecture. There are plenty of things to see and do in London, and whether it's the first time you're going or going back for another trip, there are several things to avoid doing in London, especially when planning for it! Follow the tips in this section to keep your trip planning seamless so you can get to London and be ready for your adventure.

Don't Forget to Plan Ahead

London has plenty of hotspots for people to venture to and tour, so planning ahead is essential to avoid the disappointment of not getting in on a particular day. By booking your tickets and time slots in advance, you will secure your place to visit some hotspots, allowing you to easily move from one place to the next rather than waiting in long lines and not seeing some things on the same day. Bonus: By pre-booking tickets to attractions, you'll likely save some money!

Avoid Overloading Your Itinerary

Don't overestimate London's size—it's a thriving city! You won't be able to see everything in one trip, so don't try to cram your itinerary full of things. Choose some of the things you must see and go into and consider booking one of those tours that can take you through some other spots!

Don't Underestimate the Weather

London's weather is unpredictable! Many travelers underestimate how hot it can get in the summer or cold in the winter. You likely won't need to pack a swimsuit, but make sure you have clothes to layer up with. At least with layers, you can shed them! You will also want to make sure you have a rain jacket on top, especially if a random downpour comes!

Don't Pay Too Much for a Hotel Room

Are you going to London to stay in a hotel room the whole time? I certainly hope not! Your accommodation is a place to relax and sleep, but realistically, you will only spend a little time there. Again, be mindful of your budget, but you don't need to spend much on accommodations knowing you won't be in the room for long during the day. You'll be too busy becoming a temporary Londoner!

Don't Forget an Adaptor

Compared to ours, plugs in the United Kingdom are vastly different—you won't even be able to use their plugs without an adaptor! Look for travel adaptors that are between 100 and 240 volts. However, it's a good idea to purchase an adaptor with a converter built into it, as some appliances require specific voltage requirements.

Avoid Going to Only Paid London Attractions

Paid attractions are great if you want to immerse yourself in London's culture and heritage—but they can consume a lot of your budget! Accessing museums and other local attractions and sites for free is another alternative to seeing London, so be sure to take advantage of those! (It should be noted that not all museums are free, but most are.)

Don't Only Stick to Central London

Central London is an excellent middle hub as it's close to many tourist hotspots, but the diverse neighborhoods around London have their charm. It's a good idea to check out many tourist attractions, but choose a neighborhood to venture out to! You'd be surprised by what you may learn and see.

Don't Forget an Oyster Card

An Oyster Card will be handy when using London's public transportation. It saves you from buying single tickets every time (plus buying tickets costs more). Oyster Cards are handy, and you can load them up as you need.

Traveling to any place in the world is truly one of the greatest gifts we can give ourselves. We live in a completely different world for a short time and make plenty of memories.

London is a spectacular place to adventure to. There are so many things to do and see; it's no wonder it is one of the biggest destinations for people to visit. Planning your trip to London does not need to be an overwhelming task. You'll feel more excited about getting there by preparing for your trip and having all your ducks in a row, especially now that you have some handy planning tips to get you started on the right path! Now it's a matter of preparing yourself for navigating London when you get there, which we will discuss in the next chapter.

Chapter 2:

London Tips and Tricks

Not many people know this, but London is a diverse country with over 300 languages spoken—more than anywhere else in the world! London has been a diverse city since the Roman era in 50 A.D. The early settlers on London's soil were invaders looking for wealth and land. Others who arrived in London were brought against their will. Some came to London to work as migrants or flee their home country's political issues. Nearly every person who set foot in London from its earliest days hoped that London would change their lives. Therefore, it's no surprise that London is as culturally diverse as it is! To Londoners, this piece of history and the cultural scene is as important today as it was then to ensure that everyone lives a high quality of life.

This little history lesson aside, we will look into navigating your way around London utilizing its transportation system. In addition, traveling anywhere also means learning how to take care of yourself as you move around the city.

Getting Around London

The public transportation system in London is one of the biggest networks in the world, using a large subway system (the tube), trains, and bus systems to get people to their destinations. There are several other ways to get around London, too, so let's look at each and how they can best service you.

The Tube and the London Overground

The London Underground, best referred to as the Tube is the subway system with 11 lines to service the city in nine zones. The subways run between 5 a.m. and midnight from Monday to Saturday, with reduced operating hours on Sundays.

In addition to the underground subways, London has a London Overground train system that takes you to the suburban parts of London. Some of these Overground stations interchange with the London Underground trains.

Using Google Maps will help you map out which trains to use based on where you want to go. Also, you can visit https://tfl.gov.uk/maps/track/tube to get more details on the London tube. The prices for using the Underground or Overground will vary based on where you're headed and the time of day.

London Buses

The iconic red double-decker buses are a convenient way of getting you around the

city (and you can sight-see from them too!) All London buses are cashless, meaning you will need an Oyster Card, Travelcard, or contactless payment to pay the bus fare, which is £1.75. If you are doing a day of bus-only travel, the price to ride is £2.25.

Docklands Light Railway (DLR)

The DLR is an innovative way to get around London because it's a driverless train

line! It connects you to the tube network and serves parts of east and southeast London. Services start at 5:30 a.m. and end around 12:30 a.m. from Monday to Saturday. On Sundays, the DLRs run from 7 a.m. to 11:30 p.m. The fares work the same as if you are riding the tube. You can pay using an Oyster card, Visitor Oyster Card, Travel Card, or other contactless payment options.

London Trams

London's tram network is called the Tramlink and runs between Wimbledon, Croydon, Beckenham, and New Addington. The first tram runs at 5:30 a.m. from Monday to Friday, 6 a.m. Saturday, and 7 a.m. Sunday. All tram services end around midnight daily.

The fares are treated as part of the buses with a flat rate of £1.75 if you pay using an Oyster card or another contactless payment option. You can also use Travelcards, but they do not have paper tickets.

Black Taxi Cabs

Black cabs are another iconic form of transportation seen around London. You can hail these cabs from the street or get one at designated spots, such as the train, bus, or tube stations. So long as the yellow sign is on, you will know the cab is available for hire.

London black cabs are metered with the fare starting at £3.20.

You can also book a cab through the Gett app or phone for a cab if you need their services.

Minicabs and Ubers

Minicabs are cheaper than black cabs, but only book these with a Transport for London license. These cabs are the best ones to take from the airports or if you need to take a longer trip by car. You cannot hail minicabs from the street.

On the other hand, Uber is sometimes the best value over booking a private car service. If you've used Uber before, you should have the app already on your phone. However, the catch is that you will want a U.K. SIM card because the drivers will not be able to phone your U.S. phone number.

Riverboat Services

London has an Uber Boat by Thames Clippers, which operates on the Thames. This service is fast and efficient for connecting you to various areas along the river, making it an excellent commuting method. However, it does not offer guided commentary, like riverboat cruises. According to *London riverboat services on the Thames* (n.d.), the popular stops for the Uber Boat by Thames Clippers include

- Millbank Pier to go to Tate Britain
- Westminster Pier to go to the Houses of Parliament, Big Ben, and Westminster Abbey
- London Eye Pier to go to the Sea Life London Aquarium, the London Eye, and The London Dungeon
- Bankside Pier to go to Tate Modern and Shakespeare's Globe Theater
- London Bridge Pier to see the HMS Belfast, the Borough Market, and The Shard
- Tower Pier to see the Tower of London and the Tower Bridge
- Greenwich Pier to go to Greenwich

- North Greenwich Pier to go to the IFS Cloud Cable Car and The O2

Visitor Oyster Cards and Oyster Cards are accepted for fare payment by the Uber Boat by Thames Clipper Services. However, you can purchase tickets using the Uber app. The fares vary based on the zone and if there are any discounts. It is free for children up to 4 to ride; otherwise, fares start at £5.20.

Woolwich Ferry is another ferry service available and is free. It connects you between Woolwich and North Woolwich.

IFS Cloud Cable Car

The IFS Cloud Cable Car is more of a ride than actually getting you to various places, but it's a fun way to see the Thames, London's skyline, the Royal Docks, the O2, and the Greenwich Peninsula from above.

You can get on the cable cars from the River's Royal Victoria Side or North Greenwich. The price is £6 for adults and £3 for children. Round-trip tickets are also available and are £12 for adults and £6 per child.

Santander Cycles

Santander Cycles is London's public cycle hire service. There are around 800 docking stations around the city with 12,000 bikes. To rent a bike it costs £1.65 per half hour. You can hire a bike using a bank card or using their app.

Driving in London

With London being as well connected as it is, you may not need a car. However, if you want to rent a car, I will warn you now that it is tricky as a U.S. driver! Londoners drive on the left side of the road, and the driver's side is on the right. So, it can feel difficult to maneuver. In addition, if you're driving in Central London, congestion charges will apply to your vehicle. These charges are applied in an effort to reduce emissions to improve air quality and are in effect from Monday to Friday between 7 a.m. and 6 p.m. and between 12 p.m. and 6 p.m. on Saturdays, Sundays, and bank holidays.

If you are going to rent a car, you will need 1) a valid driver's license and passport, 2) valid insurance (which includes your travel insurance and car hire insurance), 3) to provide the address of where you will be staying, and 4) credit or debit card

Travelers should be at least 23 and have been driving for over a year.

As for driving around London, we checked off the congestion charges. Here are some other things to note:

Speed limits: You will see that speed limits are listed in kilometers instead of miles. You will want to ensure you follow the speed limit, as some roads have speed cameras.

Pedestrian crossings: Crosswalks are marked by zebra crossings with stripes and yellow flashing lights. Crosswalks are busy, so be mindful of pedestrians and yield to them.

Bike lanes: There are designated bike lanes for cyclists. Be sure to avoid driving in them and double-check that no one is coming before opening your door.

Yellow box junctions: Yellow box junctions have crisscrossed yellow lines painted on the roads. You will see these in four-road intersections or in front of emergency service stations (fire and ambulance). Drivers are not allowed to stop in these boxes as they are designed to let through traffic pass to avoid traffic jams or to make way for fire or ambulance services. You will get a penalty charge notice if you get caught blocking these.

Motorways: There is no fast lane on motorways. You should only use the left lane to overtake another vehicle.

Roundabouts: Roundabouts are common in London. Traffic drives clockwise around them. As you do in the U.S., yield to the traffic approaching from your right and use your indicators to signal your exit.

Tolls: London has one toll road where Dulwich is. All cars driving along it must pay £1.20 by cash or card.

Plane Travel

You probably won't need a plane to move around the country. Plenty of trains will take you to other parts of England. However, if you want to fly somewhere, researching which airports outside of London will be helpful, and you may want to look for budget airlines.

What NOT to Do While Getting Around

London is a busy place with a lot to do. But don't get caught making these mistakes!

Don't Rush on to the Train—Wait for Passengers to Exit

A common sense etiquette in every city, but an important one nonetheless: There is nothing more aggravating than trying to get off the train while others are pushing their way on. Wait for passengers to get off before boarding.

Don't Eat on Public Transport

Eating and drinking on London's public transportation is prohibited. This helps to keep the transportation clean and less smelly.

Don't Expect Cell Service on the Tube

If you're taking the Underground tube, there is no cell service! Make sure you have an offline map downloaded or something that can help to direct you.

Don't Ignore the Signs in London

There are signs everywhere in London, making it a city optimized for tourism. If you are looking for signs to get you to some major attractions, keep an eye out for signs that will point you in that direction. And if you're still confused, ask someone for help.

Don't Opt to Take Minicabs

Black cabs are a better car service as the drivers are required to know the streets of London. Minicabs, though a cheaper alternative, are not always regulated, and the drivers often rely on GPS.

Don't Take the Tube Everywhere

Subway systems are an excellent way to get from point A to point B efficiently, but don't take it everywhere. If you're underground frequently, you'll miss some of the beautiful sites of London. Walk as much as possible in neighborhoods and take the tube to cover the longer distances between places.

Don't Forget to Use an Oyster Card

The Oyster Card is the primary form of fare payment. Using this can save you money, especially if you need to take transfers in between.

Don't Use the Underground During Rush Hour

Rush hour is a nightmare in almost every major city. Trying to take the tube during rush hour will be one of those nightmares you want to avoid, especially if you're touring London in the summer when it's hot. Avoid taking the tube between 7:30 a.m. and 9 a.m. and from 5 p.m. to 7 p.m.

Don't Forget Comfortable Walking Shoes

Expect that you will cover a fair amount of ground in London, and the last thing you want to do is trek around in uncomfortable shoes. Be sure to wear comfortable sneakers that are light to walk around the city.

Staying Safe

Being safe no matter where you are in the world is important. However, tourists are a prime target for pickpocketing, petty theft, and scams. That doesn't mean traveling to London is an unsafe adventure. It just means you must remain vigilant of your surroundings, even when London's beauty sweeps you up.

Personal Safety

Keeping yourself (and your family safe) while in London starts with being cautious. If something seems off or not right, walk away. That goes without saying that this is common sense and something you would do at home or in any big city, but you don't want to put yourself at risk when you're supposed to have the time of your life!

That said, figuring out your way around London is another good way to keep you safe. We all can take a wrong turn and perhaps end up in Knockturn Alley instead of Diagon Alley because we mispronounced the latter when using the floor powder (just kidding). Still, one of the ways to get around safely is to plan your trip so you know where you need to go and what stops to get on and off because, unfortunately, Hagrid may not be there to help you get out of those dark alleys.

As you move around the city, keep your belongings safe. If you don't need your phone, put it away, as it is one of the easiest items for someone to snatch out of your hand. Keep your bags in front of you and your arms covering them when you enter and leave buses, the tube, and anywhere else. If you carry a belt bag, a neat hack is to use a zip tie to keep the buckle together.

Emergency and Assistance

One of the best ways to avoid needing assistance is to take caution ahead of time. Make sure someone you know is aware of your itinerary and has your contact information, including your cell phone number, email, the address of where you'll be staying, and a phone number to the accommodation.

If you do find yourself in a situation where you require emergency services (police, ambulance, or fire brigade), the number to remember is 999 (be sure to highlight and bookmark this page). Calling 999 will put you in touch with a call center (the same as when we call for emergency services in the U.S.). If you require police assistance but it is not an emergency, the number to contact them is 101.

If you need assistance from the U.S. Embassy, it is at 33 Nine Elms Lane. They can provide several services to U.S. citizens, including legal services, medical services, help contacting family, and acquiring a new passport should you lose yours or it gets stolen

Medical services are free to U.K. residents, but they likely won't be free to tourists (unless in an emergency). Purchasing travelers' insurance to cover you if something happens and you require medical care is advisable.

Safety: What NOT to Do

You should avoid several things when trying to keep yourself safe, so let's jump right into them so you are prepared and aware.

Don't Fall for Tourist Scams

With London's tourism on the rise, it is no surprise that tourist scams have also risen. Here are the ones you should be wary of:

Fake theater tickets: Leicester (pronounced like "Lester") Square is a common spot for ticket scammers and scalpers to mingle. These guys will try to sell you fake tickets to a West End show with tickets below market price. Yes, cheap tickets are tempting, but it's too good to be true, and more often than not, you'll be scammed. If you intend to see a show, buy tickets through the official sites or at a box office.

ATM cameras: The ATM scan targets everyone, not just tourists. People have reported seeing cameras set above the PIN pad to record your PIN, leading the thieves to steal directly from your bank account. Using one inside a bank is better if you need to get cash.

Fake charities: If you get approached by someone asking for a charity donation, be sure they are a legitimate charity! Fake charities are often around where the real ones are. To have a charity in London, they must have a registration number and a collector's permit. Before you donate, ask them to provide proof of the charity's legitimacy.

Pickpockets: Pickpockets are always on the lookout for unsuspecting tourists. They love to hang around Leicester Square, Oxford Circus, Trafalgar Square, and on the tube to steal things from people. Always watch your belongings; when possible, put your bag in front of you where they cannot reach your items.

The wandering waiter: This scam is less well-known. However, a fake server will approach people waiting for a table. He will offer you a table if you give him your credit card for a security deposit. Restaurants and pubs don't do this, so don't hand over your credit card, or the fake waiter will run off with it in seconds!

Taxi scam: The taxi scam frequently happens to people walking toward Paddington station. A "taxi" driver will stop and inform travelers that the Heathrow Express service is not running. This is fake, of course. If you fall for it and get in, you'll pay for a costly taxi ride to the airport. Make sure to check with the station authorities before getting into the car. Also, ensure the taxi is legitimate with the proper credentials.

Don't Leave Your Bag Unattended...Ever

Leaving your bag unattended is like asking thieves to sweep in and steal your bag. Likewise, if you leave your bag unattended while on the tube, bus, or any other mode of public transportation, chances are the bag will be flagged as suspicious, causing a security alarm.

In addition to not leaving your bag unattended, be mindful of where your belongings are, and don't leave your bag or wallet open. Pickpockets are always looking for opportunities to take things, especially from people unaware of their surroundings.

Don't Start an Unwanted Conversation

The Brits are reserved; the last thing they want to do is talk with someone randomly on the tube. At a pub? Sure, go for it! But if they are minding their own business, such as reading, avoid approaching them (unless you're lost).

Don't Buy Street Meat

If you've been out to a club or a pub and are on your way home, don't buy street meat from a vendor. These guys are very unhygienic in their practices, and the chances of you getting food poisoning are high (which is a major damper on your travels).

Don't Swim in the Thames

The River Thames might look inviting when the summer days are hot, but it's not something you want to jump into. Not only is the river filthy, but it's also a main waterway for boats! Don't jump in there. Instead, find an outdoor swimming pool like the Serpentine Lido if you're looking for ways to cool off.

Respectful Behavior and Cultural Etiquette

London is known for being a classy city. Knowing how to adapt to their cultural etiquette (and doing so respectfully) will go a long way—especially since their etiquette (at times) is a little stricter. The best way to do this is to immerse yourself in the locals. Be observant of how they act so you can navigate your way and blend in with the Londoners.

How to Interact With Londoners

One of the first things to remember when interacting with Londoners is not to put on an accent. Sure, it might be cute back at home, but in London, they find it annoying (and prepare to be ridiculed). Talk as your authentic self.

With that important lesson out of the way, interacting with Londoners is straightforward. Remember your manners (please and thank you), don't be rude at the table, stand on the right while on the escalators, don't hold eye contact for too long (or strike up a random conversation), and remember to stand in the queue when waiting for everything (including the bathroom).

Interacting with Londoners does not need to be a complicated affair. By acting respectfully, you won't stick out like a sore thumb while navigating the city.

London's Historical and Sacred Sites

London is full of rich history, and we are so lucky to be able to witness it! But, as they are there for us to view and learn from, it's important to understand the rules before you enter the site. Some places don't allow photography (or flash photography), and you may need to remove your shoes if you are going to some religious sites. If you are ever uncertain, find someone to ask. You may also need to dress a certain way to enter a holy place.

Remember that you are a visitor to these sites, and it is a privilege to enter the premises, not a right. You are not entitled to everything you want, even if you have paid an admission fee.

London's Dining and Culinary Etiquette

Dining in London may not seem like it differs from here in the US, but you'd be surprised by their differing customs and table manners. For one thing, if you are staying at a bed and breakfast, you should remember that the Brits always wait for everyone to be served before they begin eating. There may not be any other U.K. residents among you for breakfast, but it is good etiquette to remember.

While dining out, if you need your waiter, raise your hand. Calling out or snapping your fingers is both rude and disrespectful. They'll see your hand and come over.

When using your knife and fork, the Brits do not switch their hands after they cut into their food to use their dominant hand. It's tricky, but they see it as an efficient way of eating instead of zigzagging. When you are done eating, place your fork and knife beside each other in the middle of your plate; your knife must be on the right side of your fork, and the fork prongs facing down. If you have a spoon, place it on the side plate.

What NOT to Do While in London

There are plenty of things you should do in London—and plenty of things you shouldn't. The best way to experience London is to try and immerse yourself in their culture and way of living. This section will cover some final tips on what not to do while in London.

Don't Forget to Book Attractions in Advance

Some attractions are popular enough that they require advanced booking, especially during peak season. Be sure to research and see what is available for the attractions you must visit while in London to avoid disappointment.

Don't Forget to Buy a London Pass

London is not a cheap city to visit as a tourist. Thankfully the London Pass is an excellent way to see many of London's iconic monuments and landmarks (including Westminster Abbey) and save up to 50% on admission. It can be pricey but worth it if you will be in London for a short period of time. Here is what it will cost per person:

	1 day pass	2 day pass	3-day pass	4-day pass	5-day pass	6-day pass	1 week pass	10-day pass
Adult	£79	£114	£129	£144	£154	£159	£169	£189
Child	£39	£54	£64	£74	£89	£99	£104	£109

Don't Overtip

To tip or not to tip? Every country is different. It's custom in the US and Canada, but in the U.K., you can either get it right or entirely wrong (which then is very awkward).

Tipping is not mandatory in the U.K. It's encouraged but not required. You may notice that many restaurants and bars will add a service charge to your bill. If you don't agree with it or feel like you were serviced well, you can have it removed. Otherwise, the rule of thumb is to tip between 10% and 15%.

Don't Stand on the Left

On escalators, especially on the Tube, stand on the right side and allow people in a hurry to pass on the left. Blocking the escalator can lead to irritation among commuters.

Don't Bring Giant Umbrellas

While London is known for its rainy days, you don't need to bring or use a giant umbrella. They take up too much space in a crowded street, and you'll annoy everyone. Pack a travel-size umbrella and wear a raincoat and wellies (rain boots).

Don't Talk About Politics, Money, or Religion

Ah, the old politics, money, or religion chatter. It should always be avoided because it's a sensitive and private topic (money) or likely to start an uncomfortable heated debate (politics and religion). Just stay away from these topics altogether. It's not something Londoners wish to discuss.

Don't Say, "Cheers, Mate!"

It may seem like a common phrase anyone can use, but the Brits hate it when people outside their country say, "Cheers, mate!" It's an overused phrase and, as a result, has lost its pleasantry.

Don't Forget to Try the Different Cuisines

Remember, London is an incredibly diverse country! Yes, they have some delicious comfort foods like beef Wellington, Yorkshire pudding, English breakfast, and fish and chips, but there are plenty of other dishes to try, including Indian restaurants!

Don't Take Pictures of People

Taking pictures in the street can be a tricky feat in London. There is a strict law about capturing photos on the street, especially if someone is accidentally caught on camera—it's seen as an invasion of privacy. Don't feel discouraged about capturing photos, but be aware of who or what you're taking a picture of to avoid being hassled by the police. You can take photos of architecture or location, but if you want to capture a candid shot of someone, get permission!

Going to London is an amazing experience with many things to see and do! However, if you have never been, you know to keep yourself (and fellow travelers) safe to have a stress-free trip. Additionally, these tips you've been given will make you feel less like a foreigner and more like a Brit!

Now that we have our essential tips and tricks down pat, we will explore London and its different regions, starting with the City of London!

Chapter 3:

City of London—Dos and Don'ts

By seeing London, I have seen much of life as the world can show. –Samuel Johnson

The City of London is not the description of the city as a whole. You are probably reading that and thinking, *what?* It is as confusing as it sounds, but the City of London lies within London, the U.K.'s capital, similar to New York City in New York State.

The City of London, or "The City" for short, is the hub for several financial institutions. Many people work in The City, but there are very few people who live in that area.

City of London's origins date back to the ancient Romans who settled in the city and called it Londinium around 43 A.D., eventually turning it into a city guarded by a wall.

An abbey was built near King Edward the Confessor's royal palace one thousand years later. The sanctuary became known as the "West Minister" (west church) as it was built on the west end side. Over the next several years, Westminster grew to be its city, and it would take hundreds of years for the varying cities in the area to unify as one.

Several pieces of the old City can be seen in the Liverpool Street Station. The City of London is sometimes called the "Square Mile" because it is one mile long by one mile wide. Interestingly, you can still see some of the original walls, and the names Moorgate, Bishopsgate, and Aldgate indicate where the entrances once were.

In many ways, the City of London operates as its own entity. Unlike the capital, London, the City of London has its own mayor, the Lord Mayor of London, who oversees the City of London Corporation. Instead of being elected by the citizens, the Mayor of London is chosen by the Aldermen, elected councilors.

What to DO in City of London

As you can see, the history and the city are complex, but it is a significant foundation for London. Naturally, there are plenty of things to see and do in City of London with its rich history, so let's explore!

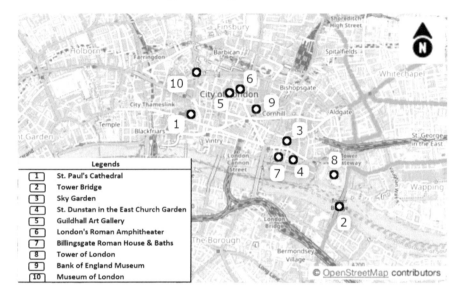

St. Paul's Cathedral

Built in 604, St. Paul's Cathedral is a familiar sight in City of London's skyline, with

its dome towering over the city. It has over 1,400 years of history (a chunk of it that many researchers still have yet to uncover). The church is a glorious building, especially with its Neoclassical English Baroque-style characteristics implemented by St. Christopher Wren following the Great Fire of London in 1666.

The dome of St. Paul's is one of the largest and tallest domes worldwide. Going to the top of the dome is an epic stair climb of 1,161 steps, but the panoramic views you'll get at the top of London and the River Thames is worth it!

It is free to enter if you wish to access the church for prayer, as it is a working church. If you want to enter and wander around, there is an admission fee of £20.50 for adults and £9 for children. You can tour St. Paul's Cathedral between 8:30 a.m. and 4:30 p.m. Monday to Friday (except for Wednesdays, where tours start at 10 a.m.). The last entry to the cathedral is at 4 p.m. However, you will want at least 90 minutes to tour the church. Tickets can be booked online through their website.

Tower Bridge

Hours of operation: 9:30 a.m. to 6 p.m. daily (last entry is at 5 p.m.)

The famous Tower Bridge (often mixed up with the London Bridge) is one bridge that will take you back to the Victorian Era. It has been a significant and defining landmark of London.

The construction of Tower Bridge began on April 22, 1894, and was completed by 1886. It officially opened with celebrations on June 30, 1894, by the former Prince and Princess of Wales, Prince Albert Edward and Alexandra of Denmark.

At Tower Bridge, you will see the City of London from another panoramic view. However, what's neat is seeing the city life from the glass floors and walkways 138 feet above the River Thames! If you time your visit, you'll see the bridge lift to let boats through!

You can buy tickets to tour the bridge on your own. However, there are also guided tours (typically on Saturdays and Sundays). The prices for Tower Bridge are as follows:

- Adults: £12.30
- Children between 5 and 15 years old: £6.20
- Disabled adults: £9.20
- Disabled children between 5 and 15 years old: £4.60
- Students 16 and up and seniors 60 and up: £9.20
- Children under 5: free

Sky Garden

Imagine walking through a garden in the sky while viewing city skylines below.

That is what Sky Garden is like. This beautiful garden is on the 43rd floor of the Walkie-Talkie building. It features floor-to-ceiling windows, a lush indoor landscaped garden to stroll through as you approach the observation decks and an open-air terrace.

It is free to visit Sky Garden. However, there is limited availability, and you must book your tickets in advance. They release tickets every Monday morning, and you will have an hour to view the gardens. However, if you want to stay longer, there are also restaurants and bars in Sky Garden for your enjoyment.

St. Dunstan in the East Church Garden

St. Dunstan in the East endured a fair amount in its lengthy 900-year history. It

was originally built in 1100 but sadly was damaged when the Great Fire erupted in London in 1866. Sir Christopher Wren rebuilt the church, finishing it as a steeple.

The church stood tall for years, but when the London Blitz occurred during World War II, it suffered immense damage when one of the German bombs directly hit it in 1941. The bombs destroyed everything in the church except for the north and south walls and, miraculously, the steeple.

When the war ended, it took years for London to rebuild. However, St. Dunstan remained in ruins, and instead of rebuilding it, the City of London Corporation turned it into a beautiful garden.

Guildhall Art Gallery

In 1885, the Guildhall Art Gallery was built to display a growing art collection in the City of London's Corporation. It didn't officially open to the public to cater to those interested in seeing unique artwork and masterpieces until 1886.

Unfortunately, when World War II began to rage across the country, much of the original gallery was destroyed during the Blitz. Thankfully, most of the gallery's art collections were put into underground storage in Wiltshire. Still, sadly, the gallery lost around 164 paintings, watercolors, drawings, and 20 sculptures due to the air raid.

When the war ended, The City built a temporary art gallery in 1946 to use as an exhibition and ceremonial space.

Nearly 30 years later, in 1985, The City decided to rebuild the gallery and add a lower level. As the gallery began to be rebuilt, the remains of the original gallery were demolished. As the architects started to dig out the remaining ruins, they came across another incredible discovery: the remains of a Roman Amphitheater. As a result of the discovery, the building was redesigned to include this historical architecture. The new Guildhall Art Gallery was officially opened to the public in 1999 by Queen Elizabeth II. This gallery has a significant history, and visitors have an opportunity to view paintings dating as far back as the 1670s to today's century.

London's Roman Amphitheater

Hidden for centuries until the Guildhall was being rebuilt, London's Roman Amphitheater was a surprising discovery. Its original walls were unearthed by archeologists digging ahead of the new art gallery's building; naturally, it had to be a part of the new Guildhall!

You can see the ruins and sand the gladiators once fought on all those centuries ago, and there is an impressive digital projection to complete the arena's gaps. It is a remarkable piece of history, especially with its timber-lined drains that have remained preserved for nearly 2,000 years!

Both attractions are free to attend and are open from 10:30 a.m. to 4 p.m. daily (with the last entry at 3:45 p.m.).

Billingsgate Roman House and Baths

Beneath The City's old cobblestoned roads lies some ancient Roman history which has amazingly survived the last 2,000 years, despite fires, conflict, and the famous Blitz of World War II.

The Billingsgate Roman House and Baths are one of these hidden treasures beneath City of London, first discovered in 1848 when construction workers were building a new coal exchange. The discovery was surprising but an important one. As a result, the remains of the baths were preserved by Victorian Londoners.

After the coal exchange shut down and was demolished, a new building was put in place, with further excavations to incorporate the cellar. Today, you can take a guided tour to see the ruins believed to have been built around 150. Public tours happen between April and November on Saturdays, and you must book your tickets in advance. Ticket prices start from £9.38.

Tower of London

The Tower of London is the City of London's iconic castle where you can get up close with the Crown Jewels, meet the Yeoman Warders, stroll among plants and flowers around the Tower Moat, and, if you dare, hear about the gruesome and haunting tales of the Bloody Tower. So much history is packed into the mighty fortress, which has stood tall for over 1,000 years!

For adults to visit the Tower of London, it is £33.60. For children between 5 and 15 years old, it is £16.80. As the operating hours vary based on the time of year, it is best to check their website for more details.

Bank of England Museum

Walk through the fascinating history of the Bank of England Museum to learn more about how its initial establishment by the royal charter in 1694 grew to become the central bank of England. In this bank, you will see ancient gold bars and manifestos of famous people who have visited the bank, including George Washington, and some Roman mosaics discovered as the bank was built. Admission is free for everyone, and the operating hours are from 10 a.m. to 5 p.m. (last entry at 4:30 p.m.), Monday to Friday. Additionally, the bank will remain open until 8 p.m. every third Thursday of the month (the last entry is at 7:30 p.m.).

Museum of London

The Museum of London is closed until 2026 when a new location will open in

Smithfield. Until then, if you wish to view some other exciting artifacts of London, you can visit the Museum of London Docklands, which has several interesting exhibitions. At this museum, you can learn more about London's hidden archaeology and the Great Fire of London, which ravaged the city in 1666. The museum's admission is free and is open from 10 a.m. to 5 p.m. daily (the last entry time is at 4 p.m.).

Things to Enjoy in the City of London

While you adventure through the City of London to see the various sites, museums, and panoramic views, remember to take the time to immerse yourself in some of the dynamic activities The City has to offer to visitors (and locals).

Walk the Historic Streets

Given that the City of London is one of the oldest regions in the country, take a walk through some of The City's historic streets. Following the City Visitor Trail will map you through the City of London, past several famous landmarks, and then a stroll through the capital. Some of these old streets you should find yourself wandering through include Watling Street near St. Paul's Cathedral, Cloth Fair, Lombard Street, Threadneedle Street and Fleet Street.

If you're unsure you want to adventure the streets on your own, join a walking tour as they will guide you through the various streets and their histories.

Leadenhall Market

Do you know the way to Diagon Alley? Leadenhall Market is a beautifully covered

market in London—and it served as the set for Diagon Alley in the Harry Potter movie franchise! You don't need to tap bricks to get in or use floor powder, but it is a site to be seen!

Harry Potter aside, Leadenhall Market has various vendors selling cheese, meat, other fresh foods, flowers, and shopping and dining opportunities. The market is open Monday to Friday from 11 a.m. to 4 p.m.

Dine in Style

If you are up for at least one fancy meal, dining in style in the City of London is a great way to go about it! There are plenty of Michelin-starred restaurants with panoramic views to dine at and historical places to hang out. The City of London has diverse food from Indian to Spanish and several other delicious eats. My recommendations that travelers must try are

Full English Breakfast: You must start your day with a classic Full English

Breakfast. This hearty meal typically includes fried or scrambled eggs, bacon, sausages, baked beans, grilled tomatoes, and toast. Some variations may also include black pudding and mushrooms. Enjoy it at a local cafe or traditional English pub.

Peking Duck: London's Chinatown, near Leicester Square, is famous for its

Chinese cuisine. Don't miss the opportunity to savor Peking Duck, a delicacy known for its crispy skin and tender meat. Enjoy it with thin pancakes, hoisin sauce, and sliced cucumbers.

Indian Curry: London boasts an incredible Indian food scene, and the City is no

exception. Try classic Indian dishes like Chicken Tikka Masala, Lamb Rogan Josh, or Vegetable Biryani at one of the many Indian restaurants in the area. Brick Lane, in the neighboring area of Spitalfields, is particularly famous for its curry houses.

Seek Out Cool City Pubs and Bars

City of London's pubs and bars have endured quite a lot over the past couple of centuries, including the Great Fire, wars, and an evolving, modernizing country. Given the City of London's age, it is no surprise that it's home to some of the oldest pubs and bars, so it feels like you're taking a step back in time. Here are some of the old pubs to check out Ye Olde Mitre, Ye Olde Cheshire Cheese, Ye Olde Watling, and Cittie of Yorke.

Several events occur in the City of London you don't want to miss out on. One of the most notable events is the Ceremony of Keys, a 700-year-old nightly tradition held at the Tower of London. The practice is part of "locking up" the Tower for the night. You must book your tickets online to attend this event, which costs £5 per person.

In addition to the Ceremony of Keys event, the annual Lord Mayor's Show is another interesting one. This event takes place when a new Lord Mayor is entering the role. It's quite the spectacle with the new Lord Mayor getting to ride in a golden carriage!

Speaking of gold, if you're interested in hunting for treasures, the Goldsmiths' Fair is a must to allow you to see inside the stunning Goldsmith's Hall.

Where to Stay in the City of London

The City of London is a great place to stay because it is a bustling financial district that quiets in the evenings and weekends. This makes it enjoyable for travelers who enjoy quieter evenings and those traveling with kids. You won't find many budget-friendly accommodations in The City, but some of these hotels are around the mid-budget range and put you close to some of the major attractions:

St. Christopher's Inn: Located on Liverpool Street near the train station, St. Christopher's Inn is a hostel with basic dorm rooms. This is an excellent option if you are backpacking, and you'll find yourself surrounded by business travelers, other backpackers, and even some locals! Guests love this hostel for its cheap continental breakfast to start your day.

Counting House: From the street, the Counting House looks like a pub, but there are 15 rooms above it, and you can expect excellent English hospitality. Start your day with a full English or Irish breakfast, then head outside to see some of the various landmarks the hotel is close to! Points of interest near the counting house include St. Paul's Cathedral, the Sky Garden, and London Bridge.

The Tower Hotel: Set between St. Katharine Docks and the River Thames, the Tower Hotel is conveniently next to the Tower Bridge. It's a beautiful hotel with a stunning view of The City, other major attractions, and public transportation.

DoubleTree by Hilton—Tower of London: Any DoubleTree by Hilton hotels are excellent for budget purposes while feeling luxurious. This DoubleTree hotel is next to the River Thames and is easily accessible to other points of interest, including St. Paul's Cathedral.

Premier Inn London Blackfriars (Fleet Street): Whether you are in the City of London for business or pleasure, the Premier Inn London Blackfriars is an ideal place to stay as it is family-friendly and central to various points of interest. You can walk to the West End to stroll through the Convent Garden, or if you're up for a show, check out a performance at the Mermaid Theatre next to it! When you're ready to settle for the day, return to your room to sleep in a comfy bed or eat a delicious meal in their restaurant.

ANdAZ Liverpool Street: Nestled in the heart of the City of London's east side, the ANdAZ Liverpool Street Hotel offers luxurious accommodation with an artistic and modern interior. You would never expect this hotel to look as stylish as it does, as the building dates back to 1884. This hotel has five restaurants, four bars, and over 250 guest rooms and suites to meet your needs after you spend the day exploring the area.

The Ned: Looking for a luxurious stay? Step back to the 1920s when you stay at The Ned, the former Midland Bank headquarters. The Ned has 250 rooms of all different sizes with a touch of the roaring 20s. It's a classy hotel throughout, and foodies love it for its 10 restaurants and their chefs' delicious creations.

London YHA St. Paul's: Once a school for the St. Paul's Cathedral choir boys, this building has now been repurposed to serve as a hostel—perfect if you are backpacking around England and Europe! This hostel has a rich history, and you'll even see some old graffiti left by the former pupils! This hostel is central to various points of interest you can reach easily on foot.

What NOT to Do in the City of London

The City of London is where everything began, so let's make the most of your trip when you venture into this area!

Don't Forget the Free Museums

There are plenty of museums throughout The City and the country, but taking advantage of some free ones is a good idea. It will save you some money, and you'll still learn about the history that started the City of London!

Don't Bring Harmful Objects to St. Paul's Cathedral

St. Paul's Cathedral is committed to keeping visitors safe. If you are found to be carrying any harmful objects, they will not hesitate to call the police.

Don't Expect Everything to Be Open on Weekends

Since the City of London is a financial district, many things tend to shut down on weekends. You will want to double-check some of the attractions you're interested in visiting to make sure they are open on the weekends.

Don't Assume Everyone Is British

London is incredibly diverse, and you'll encounter people from all over the world. Don't make assumptions about someone's nationality or background based on their appearance.

Don't Forget to Mind the Gap

The famous "Mind the Gap" warning is there for a reason. Be cautious when getting on and off the London Underground to avoid accidents due to the gap between the platform and the train.

The City of London is rich in history, especially since it's the foundation of the country's capital. Going through the City of London is a walk down memory lane, seeing ruins from the Roman Londinium to the ruins from the Great Fire of London and the Blitz. There is so much to discover and learn about London in The City, and it's one area in which you should spend at least a day.

Moving over to Central London, you will find yourself immersed in the heart of the country's capital. Central London has many beautiful sites, little nooks to discover, and many things to experience. Adventuring through this thriving part of the country will start to feel more like a true London trip.

Chapter 4:

Central London—Dos and Don'ts

H aving explored the City of London, are you ready to venture further into the captivating realm of Central London, where iconic landmarks, diverse neighborhoods, and cultural treasures await your discovery?

The City of London is an integral part of the country because it's where the foundation of the thriving London we know and love today began. Without it, it's hard to imagine what London's capital would look like! Like The City, Central London is full of history, thanks to the Romans starting a settlement in 43 A.D.

Since its inception all those centuries ago, London has evolved significantly. They have seen monarchy changes, wars that left the country in ruins, and natural disasters (the Great Smog of London) and have recouped from it all. Central London is a busy part of the city, and it can feel intimidating to tour around it, but don't let that stop you!

What to DO in Central London

With Central London being a prominent part of London, many people picture it when they hear London, and it may feel overwhelming to think about what you should do in Central London. Many people want to see and explore many obvious things, so let's get into some places you should not miss!

Westminster

Westminster is undoubtedly one of the areas many think of when London comes to mind—especially with the recent loss of Queen Elizabeth II and the coronation of His Majesty The King. In this neighborhood, you will be delighted by the historical sites, the oldest institutions, beautiful parks, and of course, Big Ben.

You'll likely wind up at Westminster Abbey as you wander through Westminster. Take in its beautiful gothic architecture that dates as far back as the 13th century. This Abbey has served the Royal family for coronations since 1066. As you continue to walk through the area, marvel at Big Ben's grand clock as it tells Londoners the time with loud chimes. When you're ready for a break and want to relax, find yourself in St. James Park and admire the lake, home to several waterbirds, or picnic under the trees.

You should walk along The Mall that leads up to Buckingham Palace—another iconic street well-known for its ceremonial purposes. If you happen to be in Central London on the weekend, The Mall is closed to traffic, making it pedestrian-friendly.

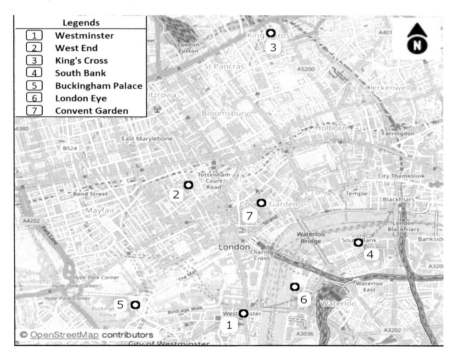

West End

The West End in Central London is famous for its shows, shopping, culture, and dining.

This is the area to go to when you want to see a show, shop along Oxford Street, visit the British Museum (which is free, by the way), and gather in Trafalgar Square, where you can see the iconic landmark Nelson's Column, the National Gallery, and the Fourth Plinth. The West End neighborhood is also home to the Royal Opera House, famous for its ballet and opera performances. You can take a guided tour to learn more about its history and entertainment dating back to 1732.

King's Cross

King's Cross is an up-and-coming neighborhood in Central London. Since the

1990s, the area has been regenerating as it declined after World War II. Over the last 30 years, this neighborhood has seen plenty of new buildings, streets, and public squares. However, it's this area that many people are familiar with due to the train station where Harry Potter and all the other witches and wizards of the U.K. boarded the Hogwarts Express at platform 9¾. Bonus tip: If you happen to be in Central London on September 1 at 9 a.m., they will announce witches and wizards to be on the train to take them to Hogwarts! Many people love gathering in the train station to hear this iconic announcement and take photos at the platform.

South Bank

On the south side of the River Thames is the beautiful neighborhood, South Bank.

The promenade is gorgeous to walk along as it offers views of Big Ben, the London Eye, and St. Paul's Cathedral. In addition, there are plenty of welcoming restaurants, pubs, and green spaces to enjoy along your adventures in the area.

South Bank also has some great vintage finds in its Flat Iron Square. Funnily, the Flat Iron Square is like a little hidden secret in South Bank, so who knows what fun vintage finds you'll come across?

If you want a space for meditating, an unusual spot in South Bank is the Tibetan Peace Garden, which opened in May 1999. The garden represents an understanding of peace and harmony among various cultures. Coming here around 2 p.m. is excellent as the park gets full sunshine, enhancing your peaceful state.

Visiting the Lambeth Palace is a great place for medieval lovers as it's the Archbishop of Canterbury's residence. It's not open for tours daily, so you'll need to find out when you can enter the palace. However, if you do get to go on a guided tour, you'll get to see the Crypt, the Great Hall, and the Chapel. There is so much more to do in South Bank, but these are some of the highlights you don't want to miss out on!

Things to Enjoy in Central London

Aside from exploring Central London, don't forget to check out some of the experiences that are a ton of fun! This section will explore many things you should consider adding to your itinerary in Central London.

Experience the West End's Nightlife

The West End of Central London has plenty of things to do when the sun sets. Many nightlifers love to check out some of the hottest bars, view the bright lights at Theatreland, and enjoy cocktails at speakeasies in Soho.

For concert or theatergoers, many people love to attend classical concerts at St. John's Smith Square, hear a beautiful choir sing in Westminster Cathedral, or catch some comedy shows at other entertainment venues in West London. Whatever you want to do, try to do at least one of these activities in the evening hours!

Family Day at South Bank and Bankside

South Bank and Bankside are excellent spots to spend the day as a family, thanks to various things to entertain all ages! If you are traveling with your family, here are some of the things you should do:

- Take a ride on the London Eye.

- Visit the aquarium animals at Sea Life London.

- Explore the dark history of the London Dungeon, complete with shows, costumed actors, and rides to bring the experience to life.

- Enjoy a picnic in Bernie Spain Gardens or Royal Festival Hall.

- Visit the Tate Museum, where you and your family can enjoy several free activities and learn about modern art.

- Have a pirate adventure aboard the magnificent Golden Hinde on the River Thames, or explore the floating museum on the HMS Belfast, a former cruiser from World War II.

Buckingham Palace

Buckingham Palace is open for 10 weeks in the summer for tourists to view the staterooms, allowing you to see what the palace looks like from the inside, where His Majesty The King and those before him have worked, lived, and entertained.

Buckingham Palace is also the backdrop for the famous free event, the Changing of the Guards.

To tour the State Rooms, Buckingham Palace is open to visitors every day except Tuesday and Wednesday. Between July and August 31, the operating hours are between 9:30 a.m. and 7:30 p.m. (the last admission is 5:15 p.m.). Between September 1 and 24, the operating hours are from 9:30 a.m. to 6:30 p.m. (the last admission is 4:15 p.m.).

Here are the ticket prices to go into Buckingham Palace. Booking in advance is your best option:

	Advance Booking	Day of Visit
Adult	£30	£33
Young adult (18 to 24)	£19.50	£21.50
Children (5 to 17) and visitors with a disability	£16.50	£18
Under 5 years old	Free	Free

Changing of the Guards

The Changing of the Guards is an entertaining event for all to see. This event is a formal ceremony where a new group of soldiers replaces the existing on-shift soldiers. It's not a simple change-over, though! They make it a complete performance, filled with commands, lots of marching, and a band playing various tunes. The entire act takes around 45 minutes. It is not something you want to miss, especially if you haven't been to London yet! The Changing of the Guards ceremony occurs every Sunday, Monday, Wednesday, and Friday at 10:45 a.m. The best place to watch it is on the steps of Victoria Memorial and the Buckingham Palace Gates.

See London From a Double-Decker Bus

The double-decker bus is one of London's most iconic modes of transportation. If you take a bus to get around, try to get a seat on top so you can see the city. However, riding in an open-top bus with hop-on-and-off options is another excellent way to see the city from above (while getting around to iconic spots). Taking a double-decker bus tour is a perfect way to see London quickly (especially if you're only here for a few days).

Ride the London Eye

The London Eye is a well-known landmark in Central London, standing tall at over

442 feet. When you reach the top, you will see a panoramic and aerial view of London. Arguably the best time to ride the London Eye is at night when the sun is setting, as the country gets bathed in beautiful orange shades, and you can see the nightlife coming to life.

If you want to avoid the lines, booking fast-track tickets will have you in the capsule and on your way up to the top more quickly!

The London Eye operates from 11 a.m. to 6 p.m. daily. Tickets start from £29.50 per child (ages 2 to 15) and £32.50 per adult (ages 16 and up); children under 2 are free. If you wish to skip the line, the fast-track tickets are £55 per adult and £51 per child.

Visit London's Museums and Galleries

London has an impressive number of museums and galleries that can capture

anyone's interest. The bonus? They are all free (which is excellent for budget purposes). Some of the museums and galleries to check out include

- The National Gallery, with over 2,300 paintings, including a collection of artwork from the Impressionists
- RHS Lindley Library, which houses some of the earliest printed books to modern-day books
- Tate Britain with art from 1500 to today
- Imperial War Museum, where you can see the wars from the perspective of those who lived through them

Book a River Thames Cruise

No matter how often you have been to London, cruising along the River Thames is a wonderful way to see London! There are several ways to cruise along the Thames, including hop-on-hop-off tours, cruises with afternoon tea, lunch cruises, the Bateaux London Dinner Cruise, which is on an all-glass boat with a three-course dinner, and Thames River Sightseeing tour, which will allow you to learn more about the history of London while seeing several iconic landmarks.

Explore the Convent Garden

Convent Market is the place for world-class shopping, dining, and attending an opera at the Royal Opera House.

Before Convent Market became a popular tourist attraction, the market was opened as a large produce, flower, herb, and root market in the U.K. Today, it houses several designer and other shops, antiques, and restaurants for everyone. You can also check out the London Transport Museum showcasing the modes of London's transportation through the decades! Convent Market is open from 10 a.m. to 6 p.m.

Savor Central London Food Experience

My recommendations for a must-have food experience in central London are

Afternoon Tea: You must experience the timeless tradition of afternoon tea in the heart of London. Indulge in a selection of finger sandwiches, freshly baked scones with clotted cream and jam, and a tempting array of pastries and cakes. Classic venues like The Ritz, Claridge's, and Fortnum & Mason offer an exquisite afternoon tea experience in elegant surroundings.

British Roast Dinner: Savor the quintessential British Sunday roast. Typically

served on Sundays, this hearty meal includes roasted meats (such as beef, lamb, or chicken), crispy roast potatoes, Yorkshire pudding, seasonal vegetables, and rich gravy. Many traditional pubs in Central London offer excellent roast dinners.

International Street Food at Borough Market: Head to Borough Market near London Bridge to explore a world of international street food. Sample gourmet burgers, artisanal cheeses, Spanish paella, Ethiopian injera, Middle Eastern falafel, and much more. This bustling market is a food lover's paradise.

Where to Stay in Central London

With a capital city home to around eight million people in 32 boroughs, where do you stay in the Central London part of London? Central London is defined by its distance to the Charing Cross train station. Staying in Central London puts you close to several points of interest, including Westminster Abbey and St. Paul's Cathedral. It's one of the most convenient areas to stay in, especially on your first visit to London. Here are some places to check out for accommodations:

SoHostel: SoHostel is one of the coolest hostels for backpackers, couples, and group travelers. Although the hostel is in the middle of Central London's action, it offers affordable rates for shared and private rooms, a restaurant, and laundry.

Astor Victoria Hostel: Another excellent hostel for backpackers as it is located about a 25-minute walk from Buckingham Palace. Guests of this hostel can have a shared or private room, make their food in a shared kitchen, and use the laundry facilities.

Best Western Buckingham Palace Rd: The Best Western Buckingham Palace Rd is a good, budget-friendly option (especially if traveling with a family). This hotel is close to the Palace, Westminster Abbey, and the Houses of Parliament.

NoMad London: New York, meet Central London. The NoMad London Hotel is a newer accommodation that opened in 2021 and is based around the New York-based brand of the same name, with an English twist. This hotel is immersed within Covent Garden, making it an excellent choice for travelers wishing to make the most of their stay in England's capital city. For dining options in the hotel, you can eat in their NoMad restaurant in a beautiful glass conservatory or grab a casual bite at their Side Hustle bar in a former police station.

The Mayfair Townhouse: This hotel has 172 rooms built across a row of townhouses. Each room has a touch of contemporary and modern pieces alongside some original art. This hotel is excellent for those traveling with families, as some rooms have interconnecting suites. In addition to this hotel being within walking distance of attractions, the Mayfair Townhouse offers personal training services and a complimentary minibar and candy.

11 Cadogan Gardens: If you're looking for a luxurious stay, 11 Cadogan Gardens is an upscale boutique hotel with various accommodation options. This hotel has 34 rooms, 22 suites, and 6 apartments embracing the building's historical roots. This hotel is ideal as it is near Buckingham Palace and a few museums and art galleries.

CitizenM London Bankside: With 192 rooms to suit the needs of leisure and business travelers, the CitizenM London Bankside Hotel has compact rooms with comfortable beds. Guests enjoy this hotel for their book and movie libraries and the ability to control technology in their rooms using an app. This hotel is an excellent option for solo travelers and those with a tighter budget. You'll also be within walking distance of the Tate Modern, Shakespeare's Globe, and the Borough Market.

Sea Containers London: Have you ever wanted to go on a cruise without going on a cruise? The Sea Containers London Hotel is one of the only hotels alongside the river. The design of this hotel makes it feel like you have set foot on a transatlantic cruise liner in the 1920s with contemporary rooms and suites. In addition to having a spa, two restaurants, and a cocktail bar, the Sea Containers London hotel has a movie theater in its basement which shows the latest movies every weekend.

What NOT to Do in Central London

With plenty of things to do in Central London, it's easy to forget about some of the things you shouldn't do when you're in this region. Let's look and see what not to do in Central London.

Don't Forget Theater Etiquette

Whether you are going to the theater in London or back home, there are some etiquette things to remember when attending a performance. The last thing you will want to do is have an awkward moment. When you are in the theater, don't bring food inside as it is disruptive for the actors and your fellow audience members, don't use your phone during the performance, and don't chit chat as it is annoying for others trying to watch.

Don't Bring Bags or Backpacks to Westminster Abbey

If you are carrying a large backpack or bag, it will not be permitted inside Westminster Abbey, so make sure to use something smaller. If you are carrying large bags or backpacks, you can leave them with the Excess Baggage Company at Charing Cross or Victoria station.

Don't Forget the Photography Rules at Westminster Abbey

Visitors can take photos in Westminster (but make sure your flash is off). However, if you are attending a service, you will not be allowed to take pictures. You are also prohibited from taking videos and using selfie sticks or tripods.

Don't Forget the Airport-Style Security at the House of Parliament

If you are touring the House of Parliament, be mindful that getting in can take up to 45 minutes, depending on how busy it is. This is because they do an airport-style security screening to ensure the safety of everyone.

Don't Go to Piccadilly Circus

Piccadilly Circus may seem like it has things to do, but it doesn't! There are a few shops and the statue of Eros, but otherwise, it's just a hub for traffic.

Don't Shop on Oxford Street

Oxford Street has several big retail names that many shopping enthusiasts love. This street has nearly every shop you can think of within walking distance of one another; naturally, it's a busy area, and it's unpleasant if you hate crowds. There are plenty of shopping alternatives to check out (and are less crowded), including shops on Carnaby Street and Brick Lane.

Don't Buy Drinks in the Mayfair Clubs

If you're looking for a place to spend a night on the town, there may be a better place than the Mayfair club district. It's expensive to get into the clubs, as are the drinks! Opt for a pub instead; the atmosphere will be more fun anyway!

Don't Dine in Leicester Square

Leicester Square is home to Theatreland and many film premieres, so it's a popular area for tourists to go to for that reason. Knowing this, restaurants are willing to increase their menu prices because they know tourists will happily pay the bill. However, the majority of restaurants in Leicester Square are chain restaurants, so you're not getting great quality food for your pound. So, if you want to experience some of London's finest dining in independent restaurants, check out Soho instead!

Don't Limit Yourself to Central London

Yes, Central London has plenty of things to see and do, but London is so much more than this hub. Don't just see all of the attractions in Central London—branch out and see other areas too! (Good thing I've got you covered for the different parts of London!)

Central London is an iconic and well-known part of the country with many landmarks, monuments, and double-decker buses. It is an excellent place to explore and experience several things, including watching the King's Guards change over to keep watch of Buckingham Palace and seeing London from an aerial view atop the London Eye. While this chapter has plenty of things you can do on your trip, don't limit yourself to Central London. There are many more things to experience, see, and do, including visiting more Harry Potter connections and the famous Abbey Road!

Chapter 5:

North London—Dos and Don'ts

W elcome to North London, the magical world of Harry Potter. Are you a muggle or still waiting for your letter via owl accepting you into the Hogwarts School of Witchcraft and Wizardry? (I'm hoping it's the latter! Maybe one day.)

Regardless of whether your letter is coming or not, North London played a significant part in filming for the eight movies. So, if you are a Harry Potter fan, a trip to North London should include seeing many of these famous locations (and much more).

What to DO in North London

While North London is the hot spot for Harry Potter fans, there are fun little towns, parks, estates, and a forest. Here is what you should do while in North London.

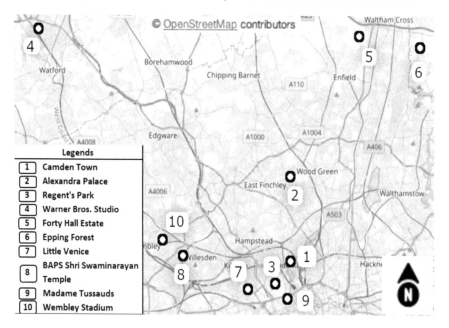

Camden Town

Camden Town has been a residential spot since 1791, but it didn't officially join London until the railway transport improved to connect it to London. What was once an industrial economic area helping grow England's capital, Camden Town has become the center for Britpop, punk, and rock music and a market that appeals to the alternative culture.

In addition to the music and shopping scene, Camden Town has plenty of things to do with your family. If you're in Camden Town during the summer, the Pirate Castle is a fun place with water-based activities that will cool you off. The London Zoo is also a fun place to test your Parseltongue skills in the Reptile House.

As you wander through Camden Town, be sure to take notice of the beautiful architecture, and its cobblestoned alleyways, and enjoy a pint of beer or cider at the Camden Pub.

Alexandra Palace

On May 24, 1832, Alexandra Palace (Ally Pally) opened in North London—but then caught fire and burned to the ground only 16 days later! Thankfully, it was rebuilt and opened two years later, and Londoners arrived in large groups for festivals, banquets, theater, and fireworks in the palace's park. As the locals enjoyed the grand space, the Act of Parliament put the Park and Palace into public ownership in 1900, allowing it to be a recreation and resort for anyone who wished to enjoy it, thus making it the "people's palace." The fun continued until World War I when it became a place refugees sought protection.

After World War I, Ally Pally became the world's first TV station, the British Broadcasting Corporation (BBC), in the 1930s. With the television station in place, the palace became a jamming station to block German radio communications from hearing where they should drop their bombs during World War II.

After World War II ended, Ally Pally became an iconic music venue where big names like the Rolling Stones, Pink Floyd, Queen, Led Zeppelin, and B.B. King played many shows.

In 1980, the palace burned down a second time but reopened in 1988, and concerts resumed; it remains a venue for concerts and other events today.

You don't need a concert ticket as a reason to go to Ally Pally. There are plenty of green spaces that many enjoy relaxing in and taking in the stunning views. Ally Pally also has several activities for people to do, including rowing boats, ice skating, or watching ice hockey. On Sundays, Ally Pally hosts farmer's markets as well. This is a great place to spend the day if you're looking to do something that allows you to relax instead of immersing yourself in the hustle and bustle of North London.

Regent's Park

Regent's Park offers visitors another scenic escape in the heart of North London. The peacefulness will make you feel like you are miles from the bustling city streets, making it an enjoyable day trip.

Once owned by the Crown, King Henry VIII used it as a hunting ground. In the early 1800s, Regent's Park would be transitioned into a pleasure garden at the request of the Prince Regent (and future King) George IV. The Prince Regent was known to be a bit of a playboy, so the Crown refused to pay for his request. The architects commissioned to work on the project (John Nash and James and Decimus Burton) found other means of financing and opened Regent's Park to the Public in 1835.

Since its public opening, the Park's 395 acres offer plenty of things to do, including

- taking a visit to the London Zoo, with over 700 animal species. (Remember, this is the zoo featured in *Harry Potter and the Sorcerer's Stone*!)
- wandering through Queen Mary's Gardens to view nearly 12,000 roses.
- playing various sports on their pitches, including football, cricket, and rugby.
- playing on one of the four playgrounds.

Warner Bros. Studio Tour London

The Warner Bros. Studio Tour London—The Making of Harry Potter will suit all

muggles, witches, and wizards! Here you will get to see the magic behind making the iconic films, learn more about what went on behind the scenes, and view many of the sets and props from the movies, including

- Platform 9¾
- the Great Hall
- the Forbidden Forest
- 4 Privet Drive
- the potions classroom
- costumes

Being able to step into the world of Harry Potter is a dream for most! Be sure to book your tickets in advance for this tour, as they sell out quickly and regularly. The tour lasts around three-and-a-half hours. Here is the pricing for the studio tour:

- Adults (16 and up): £51.50
- Children (5 to 15 years old): £40
- Family: £160
- Children under 4 are free, but they must have a ticket booked

Forty Hall Estate

Forty Hall Estate is a great spot for history buffs. This estate was built in 1632 by the former Lord Mayor of London, Sir Nicholas Rainton, with a walled garden, formal and informal gardens, lawns, meadowlands, and a lake. The house is a fine example of medieval and modern style with beautiful Jacobean era (March 1603 to March 1625) architecture.

While wandering through the estate, you can learn about Sir Nicholas Rainton's life and explore the gardens. Visitors can take a guided tour of the estate for those with special interests, which can deepen your understanding of the historic hall. If this interests you, contact Forty Hall to arrange the tour.

This admission to the museum is free and is open from Thursday to Sunday between 11 a.m. and 5 p.m.

Epping Forest

Lose yourself in nature at Epping Forest, a 6,000-acre woodland that's been

around for centuries. Before it became the "People's Forest," Epping belonged to Queen Victoria, and only a handful of people were allowed on its land until she dedicated it to everyone in 1882.

The forest is home to several animal, insect, and bird species in addition to bogs and marshes, heaths, and ancient woodland. Epping Forest also has two Iron Age earthworks, Loughton Camp from 500 B.C.E. and Ambresbury Banks (700 B.C.E.). This is a beautiful place for outdoor enthusiasts hoping to get some hiking in on their trip.

Little Venice

The quirky area of Little Venice is home to an eclectic mix of waterside cafés, pubs,

and restaurants around Warwick Avenue in North London. This is an excellent area for a morning, afternoon, or evening stroll to see the man-made waterways that connect the Grand Union Canal and Regent's Canal. (Just make sure that when you are strolling along the canal you stay on the left side, as that is the flow of pedestrian traffic.)

While in Little Venice, taking a small boat trip is a must. Sure, it's nothing like taking a gondola ride in Venice, but you will see boats decked out with decor, colors, and various styles! These boat tours will provide more history on the area as you float down the canal.

If you're traveling with kids, the Puppet Theatre Barge is a perfect spot to stop at. They perform various shows for the enjoyment of all young ages and those that are young at heart.

Lastly, if you're up for a picnic, bring a blanket and hang out on the immaculate green lawns of Rembrandt Gardens, named after one of the Netherlands' famous artists when they donated 700 tulips to London to celebrate their 700th birthday.

BAPS Shri Swaminarayan Mandir

Hidden in plain sight in Neasden, a northwest neighborhood in North London, the BAPS Shri Swaminarayan Mandir is an incredible Hindu temple that all travelers should see. This beautiful temple is fully carved out of over 5,500 tons of Indian and Italian marble and Bulgarian limestone, with some areas standing 70 feet high!

You would think that because the temple was carved out of stone, it is centuries old, but it is not. The construction for the temple began in 1993 and, amazingly, was completed in 1995! It is as impressive from afar as it is up close and open to people who celebrate all sorts of faiths year-round.

Unless an exhibition is taking place, the temple is free to enter. The operating hours are from 9 a.m. to 6 p.m. daily.

Madame Tussauds

Hours of operation: 9 a.m. to 5 p.m. daily (last entry is at 5 p.m.)

Madame Tussauds is a fun attraction to step into the spotlight with hundreds of well-known celebrities, Royals, and superheroes—in wax form. Madame Tussauds displays over 400 waxworks throughout the exhibit. You can walk the red carpet, step inside the "Royal Palace," measure up against some of the greatest Marvel Superheroes, and immerse yourself in a Star Wars experience. The displays are impressively life-like and fun to do with the family!

Ticket pricing varies per day and availability, so it is best to look on the website to get information. If you book your tickets in advance online, you will also save money.

Wembley Stadium

Wembley Stadium is home to some of the most epic football games, concerts, and other sporting events.

Wembley Stadium has been around for 100 years! It opened in April 1923, and *since its opening, it has had some incredible football moments, including hosting the 1966 World Cup, where England won!* It wouldn't have had as many epic moments had it not been for civil servant Sir James Stevenson who suggested the stadium remain open after its initial purpose of being the British Empire Exhibition in 1924 since the ground was where football had been played since the 1880s.

While Wembley is best known for football matches and concerts, it was also the venue for the London 1948 and 2012 Olympics and the 2015 Rugby World Cup. When the National Football League (NFL) ventures over the pond to play some exhibition games, they use the stadium too.

Most notably, Wembley Stadium hosted the iconic 1985 Live Aid concert, where Queen headlined, and Freddy Mercury blew the crowd away. Since then, music fans have filled the stadium to see big acts, including Taylor Swift and Ed Sheeran.

Outside of its events, Wembley Stadium offers guided tours (which can be a hit or miss depending on your interest in football).

Things to Enjoy in North London

North London has plenty of things to do and see, which is why it's one of the coolest parts of England's capital! Here are some things to enjoy and experience while hanging out in North London.

Stroll Around Hampstead Heath

London can sometimes feel like a concrete jungle with thousands of buildings, but as you have seen, plenty of places can take you away from the boxy building feeling and allow you to breathe fresh air. Epping Forest is one of those great places to do

that, but so is Hampstead Heath. Several miles of forests and grassy areas make it a wonderful place to walk and picnic while enjoying some great views of London. If you're looking to take a dip to cool off in the summer, Hampstead Heath also has some pools where you can swim.

View the Sights From Primrose Hill

Primrose Hill is a part of Regent's Park, with several views across the city. Many

duels and prizefights took place before it became a space for viewing pleasure. Now, it is the home of Shakespeare's Tree, which was planted in 1864 to mark the 300th birthday of the famous writer. From the top of the hill, you can get a beautiful panoramic view of the City of London, Canary Wharf, and various other towers and houses to the west.

Walk Across Abbey Road

It's one of the most iconic pictures in British pop-rock history: John Lennon, Paul

McCartney, Ringo Starr, and George Harrison walking across Abbey Road. Today, it's one picture that thousands of people love to recreate. A webcam takes pictures to capture people walking the crosswalk, so be sure to wave and look for your photo on their website!

Abbey Road is famous for more than just the crosswalk, though. In April 1969, The Beatles came to this street to record their final album of the same name at Abbey Road Studios. There is little to see in the studio, but you can take a photo of the building's exterior and shop for merchandise in their shop.

Must have food in North London

Salt Beef Bagel: Head out to Brick Lane's famous Beigel Bake for a classic North

London experience. Their salt beef bagels are legendary—tender, succulent beef piled high on a chewy bagel with optional mustard or pickles. It's a must-try, and Beigel Bake is open 24/7.

Turkish Meze: Explore the bustling streets of Green Lanes in Harringay, known

as "Little Cyprus" for its vibrant Turkish community. Try a variety of delicious meze dishes, including hummus, falafel, grilled halloumi, and doner kebabs, in one of the area's many Turkish restaurants.

Ethiopian Doro Wat: Visit an Ethiopian restaurant in the Kentish Town or

Camden area and savor Doro Wat, a spicy chicken stew served with injera, a spongy sourdough flatbread. Ethiopian cuisine offers a unique and communal dining experience.

Korean BBQ: Discover the flavors of Korea in North London's Korean

restaurants. Korean BBQ is a popular choice, where you can grill marinated meats and enjoy them with a variety of banchan (side dishes) and lettuce wraps.

Go to the Freud Museum

Hours of Operation: Wednesday to Sunday from 10:30 a.m. to 5 p.m.

The Freud Museum was once the home of the famous Sigmund Freud, the Austrian neurologist who founded psychoanalysis theory to understand better how the mind works to help people in mental distress.

During World War II, Freud and his family sought refuge in London when Vienna became Nazi-occupied in 1938; he brought his library papers, antiquities, furniture, desk, and famous couch when he moved. Sadly, he only lived here for a year, as he died in 1939. However, his daughter, Anna, lived there until she died in 1982.

As you walk through his house, you will see his library and study, which has remained as he left it. You will also see the dining room, explore the family tree, and view photographs on the landing and in Anna's room, where you can see her work on child psychoanalysis. Here are the ticket prices:

Adults	£14
Young persons (from 12 to 16 years old)	£9
Children under 12	Free

Explore Highgate Cemetery

Hours of operation: From March until the end of October, Highgate Cemetery is open daily between 10 a.m. and 5 p.m. (the last entry is at 4 p.m. on the west side

and 4:30 p.m. on the east side). From November until the end of February, the cemetery is open from 10 a.m. to 4 p.m. (the last entry is at 3 p.m. on the west side

and 3:30 p.m. on the east side). As this is a working cemetery, some areas may be restricted during funeral services.

Visit a cemetery? Are you mad? Nope! Highgate Cemetery is a famous burial ground in London for many good reasons, as it is the final resting place for many well-known philosophers, writers, and musicians, including

- Douglas Adams, author of *The Hitchhiker's Guide to the Galaxy*
- poet Christina Rossetti
- Leslie Hutchinson, one of the biggest cabaret stars
- philosopher Karl Marx

Aside from some notable names, the Gothic gravestones and architecture are impressive, and walking through the cemetery is peaceful. You can purchase tickets online or at the gate. However, they do not accept cash. The pricing is as follows:

- adults: £10
- children between 8 and 17 years old: £6
- children between 0 and 7 are free

If you only want to see the east side of the cemetery, reduced ticket prices are available, and are as follows:

- adults: £4.50
- children between 8 and 17 years old: £0.50
- children between 0 and 7 are free

Explore Camden Passage and Other Shopping Areas

North London has plenty of shopping places to check out. Camden Market has over

1,000 stalls selling vintage clothing, antiques, and jewelry. When you're done shopping (or need a quick break), stop for food at a stall selling international cuisine or for a drink at a bar.

Alexandra Palace hosts a farmer's market every Sunday from 10 a.m. to 3 p.m., where you can buy artisanal bread, fresh produce, meat, cheese, street food, and crafts.

If you're looking for other great vintage finds, head to the North London Vintage Market in St. Mary's Parish Hall. This market happens every Saturday between 10:30 a.m. and 4:30 p.m. You can find various vintage clothing, accessories, housewares, and jewelry pieces. The traders love sharing their knowledge on the pieces, too!

Islington Farmers' Market happens every Sunday from 10 a.m. to 2 p.m., selling baked goods, fish, fresh produce, meat, and more.

Where to Stay in North London

Staying in North London will put you in some of the busiest areas, thanks to the vibrant and historic neighborhoods. However, it's also a well-located area with plenty of public transportation to link you to other parts of the city. Staying in North London is excellent if you want something different and don't want to be immersed in the busiest parts of London.

Staying in Islington

Islington is a lively neighborhood in North London, four miles from Central London. While primarily residential, Islington has some beautiful landscapes and historic Victorian and Georgian townhouses. Here are some of the places to stay in Islington:

DoubleTree by Hilton: Located a short tube ride away from Camden and the British Library, DoubleTree by Hilton is an excellent hotel if you are traveling with your family. In addition to serving full breakfasts, the DoubleTree hotel has a rooftop bar you can enjoy in the summer.

The Rookery: Set within a row of houses from the 18th century, this four-star hotel has some charming rooms, antique furniture, and a lovely library to hang out in. It's close to the City of London and St. Paul's Cathedral.

Staying in Camden Town

Camden Town is another perfect option to stay in North London, primarily for its vibrant energy among the mix of residents in the area. With its diverse neighborhood, Camden Town has something for everyone, including the Camden Market, various cafés, street food, shops, and venues. Here are some of the places to look at if you want to stay in Camden Town:

Holiday Inn London Camden Lock: Located on the waterside of Camden Town, this mid-range priced hotel is next to London's Camden Lock. This hotel is central to several restaurants, music venues, markets, London Zoo, and Regent's Park.

York & Albany Hotel: The York & Albany Hotel is an upscale boutique hotel with unique rooms with high ceilings and a fancy four-post bed. Each room has a private entrance and terrace for your enjoyment. In addition, this hotel is near all of the major attractions in North London and has a Gordon Ramsay restaurant for fine dining.

The Standard London: Once the town hall for Camden, The Standard London offers a variety of interesting suites with bathtubs on the private terrace. They have unique features, including a library lounge, a sound Studio, and fine dining where Chef Peter Sanchez-Iglesias shows off some live fire cooking in his Decimo restaurant.

Point A Hotel London King's Cross: This hotel is five minutes from King's Cross Station and is near several other attractions, including the British Museum. Point A Hotel's rooms are spacious and modern, and a continental breakfast is served each morning.

Staying in West Hampstead

West Hampstead is an excellent spot if you are looking for ways to live like a local while traveling. Bookshops and bakeries are among the pretty residential streets, allowing you to get a feel of what living in West Hampstead is like (especially as most of the accommodations here are apartment-style). Here are some places to check out:

Charlotte Guest House: The Charlotte Guest House has 40 bedrooms and apartments with mini kitchenettes for your convenience. This accommodation is steps away from various attractions of the lively high street.

Anchor Hotel: Anchor Hotel is a family-run hotel in a residential suburb of West Hampstead, close to Hampstead Heath. This hotel is budget-friendly and about 15 minutes from Central London by the Tube.

What NOT to Do in North London

Before heading out to North London, it's well worth taking these tips to ensure you have an enjoyable experience and time there.

Don't Forget Camden Town Tube Closes

Camden Town's tube station is one of the busiest stations on the weekends when people are venturing out that way. As a result, the station closes on Saturdays and Sundays during peak hours, and you won't be able to get in; you can still get off and make connections to other tube trains, though. You will want to factor in the closure if you are going to Camden on the weekends to return to Central London, or else you'll need to catch the tube at a different station.

Don't Forget These Harry Potter Tour Tips for Kids

The Harry Potter tour is a dream for all Harry Potter fans. But if you're traveling with young ones, you should consider the following:

- There is a ton of walking and waiting.
- The tour has a lot of displays, and if your kiddos don't care to look at things, this may not be the best attraction to spend money on.

Don't Forget These Rules in Epping Forest

Epping Forest attracts many visitors seasonally, but here are some of the things not to do while exploring the woodlands:

- Don't swim in any of the lakes or ponds.
- Don't have a barbecue or bonfire in the forest.
- Don't use a metal detector without approval.
- Don't fly a drone.
- Don't forage for mushrooms or anything else.

Don't Forget to Go to a Redemption Café

Redemption cafés are an impactful way to support prisoners or people at risk of offending by providing coffee industry training. These cafes help these individuals build skills to gain meaningful work.

Don't Ignore Local Street Art

North London, particularly areas like Shoreditch and Camden, is known for its vibrant street art scene. Admire the artwork, but don't deface or vandalize it.

Don't Skip the Local Markets

North London has several fantastic markets, such as Camden Market and Portobello Road Market. Don't miss the opportunity to explore them and support local vendors.

North London is another vibrant area of England's capital with so much to see and do, especially with the various Harry Potter hot spots! While in North London and after you have finished practicing your magic for the day, check out the markets and neighborhoods and explore the parks and gardens. North London may not be the exact area that comes to mind when you think of London, but this chapter has given you plenty of notable landmarks and attractions that create this vibrant region.

East London is another area known for its theater and creative scenes. This area is constantly evolving, and there is always something to see and explore.

Chapter 6:

East London—Dos and Don'ts

E ast London is famous and infamous, thanks to people like Charles Dickens and Jack the Ripper. It is a community with a rich history, spray-painted murals, art clubs, and museums with shabby fronts. East London's look represents those famous people who stomped its once cobblestoned streets. For famed poet and playwright William Shakespeare, East London was his home.

Shakespeare is well known for his plays. But until recently, his original "wooden O" stage, known as the Curtain Playhouse, seemed lost and forgotten after it was dismantled in the 17th century. This stage is where it is believed *Romeo and Juliet* and *Henry V* debuted.

Its unearthing in 2012 was an impressive find for the Museum of London Archaeology and created excitement within the Shakespearean community. Being able to see something that was significant in the performing arts up close was a miraculous discovery after all those years.

The Museum of London Archaeology is repurposing the remains they found in the Curtain Playhouse for an exciting new museum opening in 2024 called The Museum of Shakespeare. This museum will have interactive elements within the ruins of the Curtain Playhouse, allowing visitors to explore the life of this writer who was and continues to be a source of influence in the English Literature world.

What to DO in East London

East London is famous for its theater and dark history, but it's also an up-and-coming area thanks to the architecture and artist studios, making it hipper. Sure, Jack the Ripper caused terror in the streets between 1888 and 1891, but plenty of other historical pieces make East London an exciting place to explore. Here are three facts not everyone knows about East London:

You're not alone if you have ever been through Aldgate Underground Station and felt some weird energy. When the Great Plague took hold of England in 1665, the bodies of those who caught the deadly disease had to be buried somewhere. That somewhere happens to be below Aldgate Underground Station, and there are thousands of bodies laid to rest in the plague pit below the tube. It's a creepy thing to think about, so try *not* to keep that in mind if you commute through here!

The Brick Lane Market used to sell exotic animals in the 1950s. When it first opened, it sold birds and dogs and later evolved to selling other types of animals, including lions, monkeys, and snakes! Don't worry—it was shut down by the Royal Society for the Prevention of Cruelty to Animals (RSPCA) in the 1970s. Today you can find some great vintage finds, food, and other knick-knacks.

Let's be honest: East London is far from elegant. In fact, East London was quite grim until the late 1900s! Funnily, one of their boroughs, Shoreditch, may have gotten its name from an old English word, *Soerditch*, which means "sewer's ditch." For what it's worth, that name was likely fitting for the rougher times of East London. With those fun facts in mind, let's explore some areas you should visit in East   London.

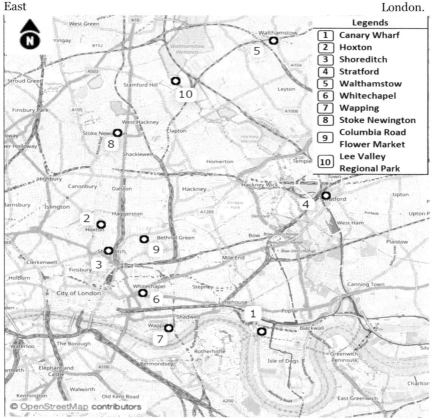

Canary Wharf

Canary Wharf is a city-within-a-city in East London. It is home to a bustling

financial district and several impressive high-rise buildings with stunning modern architecture along London's Docklands.

As you explore Canary Wharf, visit the Museum of London Docklands. This museum shares the history of London's docks, the trade history, the Docklands during the War, and the darkness surrounding London's Sailortown. The entrance into this museum is free.

When you're done at the museum, stroll around the roof garden of Crossrail Place. The garden is filled with plenty of plants and specimens from around the world, including bamboo from China and Japanese maples. There are also plenty of street food vendors within the complex with various international dishes.

Sit in one of Canary Wharf's three parks when you're ready for a break. These parks are Canada Square Park, Mudchute Park and Farm, and Jubilee Park.

Hoxton and Shoreditch

Hoxton and Shoreditch are a five-minute tube ride from London Bridge. These areas are well-known for their hipster vibes and graffiti murals, making them a popular place for artists to live in East London.

Many people love to go to Shoreditch, not just to view the street art, museums, and galleries but to check out the various markets at Brick Lane, The Old Spitalfields Market, The Sunday Upmarket, and the Columbia Road Flower Market. For nightlife, Shoreditch knows how to throw a party with its circus-themed pubs and comic book bars.

Meanwhile, Hoxton was once the center for trading furniture during the 19th century and home to the Britannia Theater until it burned down. The lease for the building was sold, and a new cinema was built in its place. That cinema was demolished sometime in 1940 to make room for a new cinema that was never built. Now it has several houses on the site and a historic plaque marking its history.

While Hoxton's area also has plenty of art galleries displaying the work of London's newer artists, you can come here to watch movies on the rooftop terrace of the Queen of Hoxton have coffee with cats at the London Cat Cafe, or enjoy drinks and a relaxing afternoon in Hoxton Square. There is no doubt that no matter which neighborhood you venture to, you won't fall short of things to do and see!

Stratford

Stratford is best known for the 2012 London Olympics, and while the London

Olympics have long since passed, tourists love to come here for some retail therapy.

Stratford's first recorded mention was in 1067. It began as a small Roman village, eventually becoming a farming area, providing several agricultural goods to London, mainly potatoes. By the 19th century, Stratford became more industrial, with more factories and workers working there. In 1839, Stratford got its railway station and eventually became a significant employer for workers to build coaches, wagons, and locomotives. The railway production arguably put Stratford on the map.

When you go to Stratford, unfortunately, you won't be able to see the buildings and structures as they have either been repurposed or demolished. However, as this area was one of the centers for the 2012 Olympics, you can see several of those buildings, go swimming in the London Aquatics Center, and shop in the huge Westfield shopping mall! If you're into bouldering (a different form of rock climbing), check out the Hackney Wick Boulder Project, where you can boulder through several problems!

Walthamstow

Walthamstow, located at the end of the Victoria Line, is an overlooked part of East London, but in recent years has gone through a significant transformation while maintaining its charm. Walthamstow has a collection of eclectic shops, a vast nature reserve, and markets.

As you explore Walthamstow, one of the places that you must visit is God's Own Junkyard. It is a free gallery with a massive collection of neon lights. It's only open on weekends, but there are so many funny signs to see!

For good pizza, grabbing a slice or a whole pizza from Yard Sale Pizza is a must! The restaurant is set in an old glass factory and serves up some of the best pizza in Walthamstow!

Speaking of old factories, a former World War I factory has been repurposed and is now home to a boutique cocktail bar, Mother's Ruin Gin Palace. Here you can enjoy over 70 different types of gins distilled from their orchards or foraged from the wilds of Walthamstow.

Whitechapel

In 1888, something sinister happened in the Whitechapel neighborhood when a

serial killer started terrorizing the area, killing at least five women in his five active years.

Whitechapel is undoubtedly best known for the infamous Jack the Ripper, but those dark days have passed, and Whitechapel has plenty of things to explore and see! For example, this area is a growing art scene. You can view several works of art in galleries displaying artwork from emerging artists.

If you want to check out where some of the bells were constructed for Big Ben, the Bell Foundry is behind creating them! You can't tour the 500-year-old factory, but visitors enjoy visiting the store to look at the different handbells, clock bells, and chimes.

With all the wandering around Whitechapel you'll be doing, you'll likely build up an appetite. It's a good thing Whitechapel has a heap of delicious places to eat, such as Treves & Hyde for some duck or beef, Pizza Union for pizza, and Grounded for poached eggs.

Wapping

Walking through Wapping will give you an exciting history lesson. Wapping was

the central point for ships to dock and unload their imported cargo until the 19th century, when more docklands started to pop up in East London. Its worst fate and decline happened when World War II was raging, with bombs impacting the docklands.

Ever since the dramatic changes, Wapping has become another up-and-coming neighborhood. As you wander through Wapping's streets, you'll see several restaurants and pubs along the waterfront to enjoy a bite or a pint. As you walk around the waterfront, be sure to visit Tobacco Dock if you're there on the weekend. This dock is where the ships carrying the imported goods would dock. It's seen several changes throughout the years, including a shopping center at one point, but now it's an area for festivals and other events.

For music lovers, going to Wilton's Music Hall takes you back to the ballroom dances from the 1820s. This place has excellent live music if you want a fun night out.

Stoke Newington

Stoke Newington (or Stokey to the locals) is a village-type neighborhood

surrounded by ample green spaces and vibrant colors.

At the time of its establishment, Stoke Newington became a safe space for Jewish immigrants who moved to East London from Germany, Russia, and Poland during the 19th century. It has changed significantly throughout the years, so there are plenty of things to see and do in this region.

While in Stoke Newington, going to Clissold Park is a beautiful place to spend the day. It has one of the best green spaces in all of England and is towered by the Clissold House, an odd-shaped house with two stories on the house's west side and three on its east. You can play tennis or wade in a pool on a hot summer day at this park.

However, if you fancy taking a dive, going to the West Reservoir Center is an excellent place to cool off! There are plenty of watersports for your enjoyment on its 23-acre lake!

For street sites, walk along Stoke Newington Church Street. This road has several shops, cafés, pubs, restaurants, and street art, which makes for a colorful stroll.

Things to Enjoy in East London

The East side of London is one of the most exciting areas to visit if you're looking for a day or two out of the busy parts of London. This section will look at the things you should take the time to Enjoy while you're in East London because of how diverse and dynamic this area is!

Admire Shoreditch's Street Art

There is no shortage of street art in Shoreditch, especially since it is a thriving artistic community. As you walk through the various streets that make up Shoreditch, you'll see some giant murals taking up the whole side of a building to smaller pieces completed by street artists. Some of the more iconic pieces to check out include

- Designated Graffiti Area on Rivington Street by the artist Bambi
- a 3D image of two octopuses enjoying a popsicle
- an image of the Mandalorian from the Star Wars franchise on Chance Street
- Lewis Campbell's *Hear No Evil, Speak No Evil, and See No Evil* on Heneage Street

Indulge in Tasty Eats at the Sunday Market

Victoria Park's Sunday market is full of fresh produce, meat, fish, and delicious street food to satisfy your taste buds. There are so many yummy eats to try as you wander by the various stalls—and they are not your basic street foods! At the market, you can snack on some pies, eat a cheese toasty (a different way to call it a grilled cheese), indulge in some pasta made in a cheese wheel, and if you're still not satisfied, enjoy a donut or other baked goods! The Sunday market happens weekly between 10 a.m. and 4 p.m.

Enjoy Slick Cocktails in Speakeasies

"Speakeasy" is a word that comes to mind when people think of the Roaring 20s and the prohibition era (1920 to 1933) in the United States, where the only way you could get an alcoholic drink was by prescription. Otherwise, it was enjoying some drinks in establishments that illegally served them. America picked up on this little trade secret thanks to England and Ireland, who practically invented speakeasies in the 19th century.

Today, buying alcoholic beverages in bars and restaurants is accepted and legal. Still, speakeasy bars have started to pop up worldwide because there is something about going back in time!

Speakeasies fit well into East London's edgy scene. These bars are cleverly hidden among other shops and offer a relaxing atmosphere with dim lighting with some classic cocktails and other beverages. Here are some of the speakeasies to seek out and try:

The Mayor of Scaredy Cat Town: From the first glance upon entry, it looks like a breakfast club. All seems normal in the world. However, if you tell the hostess, "I came here to see the Mayor," you will be brought through a refrigerator door and into the speakeasy. The address for The Mayor of Scaredy Cat Town is 12-16 Artillery Lane, London, E1 7Ls.

NightJar: Hidden in plain sight between two cafés on City Road is a narrow wooden door with a bird engraved into a bronze square. This narrow wooden door leads you to NightJar, a swanky speakeasy furnished with plush red seating and wooden décor to recreate the 1920s. This establishment has great cocktails you can enjoy while listening to live jazz, blues, or folk music. Anyone could walk by NightJar's door and not realize it's there. But when you do, you're in for a fun night out! The address for NightJar is 129 City Road, London, EV1V 1JB.

Discount Suit Company: Set in the basement of an old tailor's stockroom, the Discount Suit Company has some cheap cocktails for your enjoyment. To find this speakeasy on Wentworth Street, look for a sign with some letters missing to spell out the bar. The address for Discount Suit Company is 29A Wentworth Street, Spitalfields, London, E1 7TB.

Stroll Through the Colorful Columbia Road Flower Market

There is something about brightly colored flowers that can brighten up anyone's

day! The Columbia Road Flower Market has 60 independent shops selling art, baked goods, vintage clothes, deli meat, and antiques alongside hundreds of flowers! It's a lovely way to spend an early morning or afternoon in East London.

Play in Lee Valley Regional Park

Spend the day playing with your family in Lee Valley Regional Park. There are plenty of activities for everyone, including getting active on the ice-skating rink, playing hockey or tennis, visiting animals on the farms, golfing, cycling, and hiking.

In addition to the activities available at Lee Valley, take the time to explore the area. You can see the 1776 scenic House Mill, England's oldest and biggest tidal mill, at Three Mills Island. Tours are available every Sunday between May and October and every first Sunday in March, April, and December. These tours are £3 per person.

Take a Jack the Ripper Tour

It's an unsolved mystery that has fascinated true crime and curious minds for years. Who was Jack the Ripper? Join an expert on the subject, known as a Ripperologist, and walk the trail of the Whitechapel murders that spanned between April 1881 and February 1891. These tours will bring you through Whitechapel as you learn about the victims and their families, hear the gory details as you visit the crime scenes, and learn about the suspects' police investigated as they tried to solve who the serial killer was. The Jack the Ripper Tour is about two hours long, and tickets start at £15.

Must have cuisine

Bagels from Beigel Bake: Located on Brick Lane, Beigel Bake is a legendary

24/7 bakery known for its freshly baked bagels. Try their salt beef bagel or classic smoked salmon and cream cheese bagel for a taste of East End history.

Salted Caramel Anything: East London is home to the famous salted caramel

trend. Try salted caramel brownies, ice cream, or salted caramel-filled doughnuts from local bakeries and dessert shops. The sweet and salty combination is irresistible.

Where to Stay in East London

Artsy East London is a great option to immerse yourself in the artist scene and the various markets. It's still relatively close to other parts of London but offers a different vibe than the City of London or Central London. Here are some great options to look into for accommodations:

Batty Langley's: Batty Langley's is a quirky hotel in the Shoreditch neighborhood. Guests of this hotel can channel their inner Sherlock Holmes and Watson as they roam through the wood-paneled hallways, relax on antique couches, and scan the bookshelves crammed with first editions. This hotel will surely leave you feeling like an aristocrat instead of a 21st-century traveler!

Mama Shelter: Located in Hackney, Mama Shelter is a nod to the 1970s and 1980s with its furnishings and trinkets. This mid-budget hotel will meet your needs as a traveler with comfy beds, making it feel like home after your adventure outside in East London. This hotel is near various points of interest in East London, including the Columbia Road Flower Market.

New Road Hotel: Stay the night (or two or three) at the New Road Hotel set in a repurposed textile factory. This hotel has several rooms available, including some that will meet your budget. This hotel is steps away from Brick Lane if going to their market is on your list of things to do!

Park Villa Boutique Hostel: If you're backpacking and looking for affordable hostels in East London, the Park Villa Boutique Hostel has private and shared rooms and a kitchen. This hostel is near the Stratford Tube Station and steps from Victoria Park.

The Stratford Hotel London: Set in the popular area of Stratford, The Stratford Hotel is conveniently located near the Olympic Stadium. Each room offers comfortable accommodations with spacious rooms and a terrace.

Hotel Saint London: Just steps away from Whitechapel, the Hotel Saint London has a roof terrace and city views while enjoying a cocktail on their rooftop bar. This hotel is a perfect stay in East London as it's still relatively central to other points of interest.

Canary Riverside Plaza Hotel: If you're looking for a more luxurious stay, the Canary Riverside Plaza Hotel can provide that! Set in the vibrant financial district of East London, you can easily access the Canary Wharf Pier and check out other buildings and attractions in Canary Wharf. Guests also have access to the Health Club, which has three floors of fitness equipment, saunas, steam rooms, and a 20-meter infinity lap pool.

DoubleTree by Hilton London—Docklands Riverside: This DoubleTree Hotel is highly rated among guests for its location. This hotel is in a repurposed 17th-century building that once built ships. Guests have the option to choose from a variety of rooms facing the River Thames, and some also have a private balcony. This hotel is near various Canary Wharf attractions you can get to by their free ferry service!

What NOT to Do in East London

East London has many things to do if you are looking for a unique excursion in the city's east end! As you walk through the various streets of East London, follow these tips to make your adventuring enjoyable!

Don't Forget About the Markets

As you have learned in this chapter, East London is a lively and trendy area. Between the artwork and different cuisines, there is a lot to do! But you should remember to attend at least one of their many markets! You never know what you may find there! Plus, you can chat with the sellers in the market stalls with antiques or other vintage finds and learn more about their origins! To refresh your memory, be sure to check out the following markets: Old Spitalfields Market, Old Brick Lane Market, Columbia Road Flower Market and, Victoria Park Market

Don't Get Confused by Cockney Slang

London is full of slang, but the Cockney ones can be pretty puzzling! Somehow "fisherman's daughter" means "water," and "apples" can mean "stairs," as in "she's gone down the apples." It's undoubtedly as confusing as it reads, especially when you've never heard it. You will find various Cockney slang words in the glossary that you might overhear. While the slang originated in East London, it also spread to South London and Essex.

Don't Forget Canary Wharf Is Pricey

Canary Wharf is making its mark on the map, and given its metropolis energy, it should come as no surprise that eating, dining, and staying here will be significantly pricey. As such, you'll want to remember this when you visit this area.

Don't Miss the Street Art and Bars in Shoreditch

Shoreditch is an eclectic area brimming with street art and interesting bars. This is one area you shouldn't miss spending the day seeking out some Instagram-worthy street art to capture images of, and then having a night out with other travelers and locals in one of the many bars.

The East side of London is not always at the top of every traveler's list of things to see and do—until they go and realize the fun energy East London has to offer everyone! East London is the place to go to satisfy your love of street art to theater, true crime to other historical pieces, and seeing some Olympic landmarks up close and strolling through one of their many markets!

With plenty more to discover in London, we will go to South London next. South London is another hipster-type area, rich with history and home to the iconic Wimbledon Stadium.

Chapter 7:

South London—Dos and Don'ts

I f it weren't for the Vicar's Oak, an ancient Oak tree in the South London neighborhood of Norwood, there would not have been a clear boundary marker between the four parishes encompassing the area: Lambeth, Camberwell, Battersea, and Streatham. Though now a tree stump, the Vicar's Oak still serves as a boundary between the existing boroughs of Lambeth, Croydon, Bromley, and Southwark, making up some of South London.

There is much to do in South London, another part of the city brimming with history. South London is somewhat of a broad term given that anything south of the Thames is, well, south. However, South London and North London are rivals! Depending on where locals were born, there is undoubtedly a cultural divide between football teams and bars, with each side saying theirs is better. Is it, though? I'll leave that to you to decide for yourself since you're an outsider and not a local to the country.

What to DO in South London

South London has often been seen as a little off the beaten path compared to the other areas of London, and that might be because it's not as well serviced via public transport as perhaps North or Central London is. But you can still get there via tube, the Overground train, or bus, getting off at stations like Wimbledon and Brixton. You'll need to map out the best way to get there once you know what places you want to visit.

When you arrive, you will find plenty of places to explore in the area with cute village-like neighborhoods and other hotspots. In many ways, South London is like its own town. Here are some things to do in South London.

Croydon

Croydon is an outer borough of South London near Surrey. This big town within South London has evidence of early existence since 809 B.C.E. However, it's best remembered for housing several estates of the Archbishops of Canterbury, the primary leaders of the Church of England.

At one point before the 19th century, Croydon served as an old Surrey market town between London and Brighton. However, as London and its surroundings grew, it would only be natural that residents would expand outwards to Croydon, especially when the transportation system began to be developed and expanded.

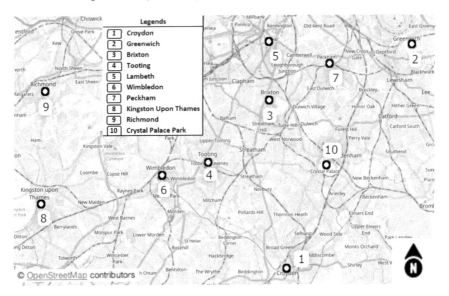

As you walk around the town, you will see plenty of nods to a town that existed long before our time, especially with Croydon Palace and Whitgift Almshouses. Croydon has become more recognized in recent years due to Adele and Jessie J attending Croydon College to perfect their singing.

There are several notable things to see and do in Croydon. One of these things is to visit the Croydon Airport Visitor Center. This landmark was the first airport in the United Kingdom, evolving from World War I. Flights out of the former airport did not begin until 1920, and the final one departed in 1959. The Croydon Airport Visitor Center exhibition will teach you about the U.K.'s air history, charting during World War I, and much more.

The Museum of Croydon is another place to explore Croydon's history. This museum in the clock tower has plenty of interactive ways to learn about the items, making it an enjoyable experience. You can visit this museum between 11 a.m. and 5 p.m., Monday to Saturday.

Since Croydon was a market town at one point, the Surrey Street Market is one to check out. Many of the vendors sell fresh fruits and vegetables. However, an artisan market runs on Sundays with live music and street theater.

Croydon has plenty of outdoor spaces for travelers looking to spend a leisurely afternoon outside. At Addington Park, you can enjoy spending the afternoon in its 24½ acres of landscaped parkland and woods. This park was once King Henry VIII's hunting grounds before the Addington Palace became a building used by the Archbishops in the summer.

Greenwich

Greenwich (pronounced *gren-itch*, not *green witch*) is a stunning riverside Royal

Borough in South London and the Prime Meridian of the World. This is one of the best places to visit in South London as it has plenty of historical attractions, museums, and markets.

The Old Royal Naval College and the Painted Hall are two must-see places in Greenwich. James Thornhill painted *The Painted Hall* between 1707 and 1726, and his masterpiece was recently restored. The tall windows, painted ceilings, and walls will take your breath away.

As for the Old Royal Navy College, this estate has 600 years of history linking to King Henry VIII, Queen Elizabeth I, Shakespeare, Queen Mary, and King William. You'll learn about the building's history as a Navy College and Royal Hospital and several key historical moments.

One of the biggest attractions in Greenwich is the Royal Observatory which played an influential role in astronomy and navigation. The observatory is home to the U.K.'s largest refracting telescope. The observatory and the attached planetarium will make for an engaging educational component, perfect for kids and adults who love learning about space!

While in Greenwich, you should climb aboard the Cutty Sark, the last surviving tea clipper. This 19th-century ship will give you an idea of what it was like to sail the seas while learning how it helped to import tea from China.

One last place to put on your must-explore list is Greenwich Park. This is one of London's oldest Royal Parks, dating back to Roman times. Interestingly, King VIII was born in Greenwich Park, and it was he who introduced deer to the park. This park is expansive and perfect for kicking a football or lazing around while enjoying a picnic.

Brixton

Brixton is one of the coolest neighborhoods to venture to, *not* just because it's the

birthplace of one of rock and roll's *biggest* stars, David Bowie. Brixton has plenty of music venues people love and is filled with various cultures.

As you walk through Brixton's streets, take notice of their street art! It's like walking through Shoreditch, but this street art is representative of Brixton's heritage. Plenty of Brixton's street art is dedicated to the arts (and even some political statements). There are specific streets to find them, so keep your eyes open as you walk because you'll never know what you may find!

As London, in general, is an incredibly diverse country, Brixton is home to the first cultural center focused on Black heritage at the Black Cultural Archives. This building gives visitors a genuine look into the experiences of the Afro-Caribbean community who were shunned and refused work when they immigrated to London following the war. These experiences are shown in a collection of letters, photographs, and other pieces of literature to illustrate the successes and struggles of many. One thing to note is that you must book your tickets in advance if you want to go to this attraction.

Book lovers unite in Bookmongers. Entering a bookstore is heaven to all bookworms, and Bookmongers offers a diverse range of books on every shelf and in every corner.

Brixton is significant in the music scene, so nightlife is a must here. The various music venues entertain all music lovers, and most bars are open late.

In the morning (following your late night), stop by the Blues Kitchen for brunch every Saturday and Sunday between 10 a.m. and 3:30 p.m.

Tooting

Okay, if you giggled a little bit reading Tooting, I don't blame you! It's somewhat

hilarious that there is a neighborhood with that sort of name, but it is a lovely family-friendly area with a cozy atmosphere and plenty of spaces to hang out!

Tooting has some hidden gems. However, one of the popular attractions for visitors is going to the railway station, Tooting Broadway (where you can get off to get to Tooting). Charles Holden designed Broadway, and its doors opened to passengers in 1926. While this does provide tube service, Tooting Broadway has several coffee and fashion shops. In addition to Tooting Broadway, Tooting Bec is another way to get into this neighborhood and boasts a unique underground design, which is worth looking at as you leave the station.

If you are in the U.K. in the summertime and looking to cool off, dip in the Tooting Bec Lido, the largest outdoor swimming pool in the country. The massive pool is a whopping 100 yards long and 33 yards wide, offers a sunbathing area, and has a café.

For great food in Tooting, plenty of international cuisine options are available, including South Asian curry and delicious dosa from India.

Learning about the various things you should do in Tooting would be incomplete without reading and learning about Bec Common. Bec Common is a large park with a stunning lake. This is a great space to have a picnic and let your kids play in the playground during the summer or enjoy some hot food and drinks at the café during the cooler months.

Lambeth

The neighborhood of Lambeth is a popular area for tourists to immerse themselves

in a culturally rich setting, likely because it is situated along the River Thames. This area is home to the Archbishop of Canterbury in the Lambeth Palace. Not many people know this, but you can visit it and walk through its ancient halls. It's stunning inside with its stone walls and rows of books in the Great Hall. Going to the Lambeth Palace will help you better understand the importance and influence the Church of England has had in the country.

One of the other popular places travelers love to venture to in Lambeth is the Imperial War Museum to experience World War I, including a walk through a trench and viewing the Holocaust exhibition. It is a grim but fascinating way to immerse yourself in a historical event that shifted the globe.

While in Lambeth, strolling through a park is a great way to get to know the area and see some beautiful high points of London. Norwood Park is one of these parks which will give you some of the best views of London on a clear, sunny day. Brockwell Park is another area that will provide you with beautiful views of the city's skyline.

Wimbledon

Wimbledon is well-known for tennis and the stars that take the courts to win the prestigious title. But aside from the famous stadium, Wimbledon has plenty of pretty parks, food, and unique stores, making it a perfect place to venture for the day.

As you walk through Wimbledon, you may see a windmill in the Common, an ample open green space. The windmill was built in 1817 and is much more spacious than you would typically think when you see a windmill. Now a museum, you can learn about the construction of windmills and how they function. In addition to learning about the history of windmills, children have the chance to try out milling. It is a cheap attraction to visit as it costs £1 per child and £2 for adults.

Tour the All England Lawn Tennis Club if you are in Wimbledon beyond the tennis matches and championship games. This tour will take you through the center court and provide a glimpse into the Millennium Building's private facilities, reserved for the higher-ranked players, media, and the trophy room. However, if you are lucky enough to be in England when Wimbledon is happening, there is nothing like experiencing the energy from the tournament, even if you can't get tickets!

One of the other best ways to experience Wimbledon is by horseback or following with Wimbledon Way. By horse, you can saddle up at Wimbledon Village Stables and ride along the Wimbledon Common's gorgeous lands. On the other hand, walking along Wimbledon Way will take you through the area's downtown, and you'll walk along to the All England Club through Wimbledon Common. This walk will bring you several noteworthy buildings, monuments, green spaces, and tennis, giving you an in-depth history lesson on what Wimbledon is all about.

If markets interest you, Wimbledon has a small farmer's market every Saturday. There are around 20 vendors who sell everything from organic honey to various produce.

While in London, it is always worth going to an afternoon tea at least once. It can be costly in some places, but in Ely's, Wimbledon's oldest department store, you don't need to break the bank for a pot of tea, mini-sandwiches, and scones!

Enjoying afternoon tea is always lovely to do with your kids, as it makes them feel special regardless of their age.

Peckham

The colorful town of Peckham has a long history, from its earliest days of being a place for wealthy people in the 16th century to an industrial area in the 18th century when it became the hub for growing figs and melons to sell at the markets. Today, Peckham is home to diverse cultures and artsy venues. This neighborhood's rich history has a different taste of London life, making it a unique place to visit in South London.

To get first-hand experience of what Peckham is all about, you're best to start adventuring along Rye Lane, the district's bustling center and one of Britain's largest British-Nigerian communities. Here you will find delicious restaurants serving up some authentic African eats.

Rye Lane also displays unique architecture as a central shopping area from its earlier days. At the corner of Peckham High Street and Rye Lane, you will see a large building and clock tower from a former department store: the Bussey Building. It will show how Peckham evolved into an artsy hotspot with theater and live music.

The artsy side of Peckham doesn't just end in Rye Lane, though. Peckham is starting to gain attention and admiration from street art lovers. You'll see plenty of that as you wander through the nooks and smaller alleys in Rye Lane and beyond. For other ways to see art exhibits, head out to Peckham Levels, a converted multistory car park with plenty of restaurants and artistic spaces to enjoy.

Kingston upon Thames

Did you know that Kingston upon Thames is one of the oldest Royal Boroughs in the country? This area was first recorded in history in the year 838 as a medieval market town and was where the first kings of England were crowned. Today, Kingston upon Thames has hundreds of unique shops, markets with themes, street performances, bars, restaurants, and cafés.

Visiting Kingston upon Thames will give you a rich glimpse into its earlier origins, especially if you begin at the All Saints Church. The All Saints Church is where England's First King, Athelstan, was crowned in the year 925. Historians argue this is where England truly began with the momentous occasion. Visitors of the church are welcome to attend their services or visit the building to learn more about their heritage gallery and see its stained glass and architecture.

No matter where you travel, palaces are always a vision of magic, transporting you

back in time. About 2 ½ miles from Kingston upon Thames lies the Hampton Court Palace, a Tudor-style building and one of the only two surviving palaces formerly owned by King Henry VIII. For history buffs who love learning about King Henry VIII, the Hampton Court Palace will share details on the King's life in a Tudor court. You will see the Great Hall, walk along the famous Haunted Gallery, and see the Tudor kitchens. It's an interesting place to get a feel for life during King Henry VIII's reign.

Kingston upon Thames has plenty of well-loved brands to shop for on a shopping excursion, including Zara, John Lewis, Apple, and other independent shops.

Finally, after all of your adventuring and sightseeing, take the time to enjoy a pint and a bite to eat at one of the pubs along the Thames as you watch the world go by.

Richmond

Like Kingston upon Thames, Richmond is another borough along the River Thames. Richmond is a great place to visit because of its beautiful views. There are plenty of cobblestoned streets leading you along some beautiful sites of the rover and various architecture. If you're walking along the river, pause and sit on the steps of the towpaths to watch the boats or enjoy a picnic in a green space.

If you want to walk through a park, Richmond Park is the largest Royal Park, housing many ancient trees and a 40-acre Isabella Plantation. In addition, Richmond Park has six original gates designed by Sir John Soanes.

Richmond is also home to the Ham House and Gardens, a 17th-century mansion

built in 1610. This home has a collection of art, furniture, textiles, and a tranquil garden covering 12 acres.

Things to Enjoy in South London

South London has plenty of sites to see and villages to explore. However, take some time to check out some of these ideas that will fully allow you to experience South London's diverse and dynamic neighborhood.

Climb the O2 Arena Roof

Are you brave enough to handle heights? The O2 is famous for hosting several

concerts over the last decade. If you dare, climb 170 feet to the top to be rewarded with some fantastic views of South London, proving that the O2 is more than just a popular entertainment complex. For those that are even braver, you may even want to bungee jump!

There are several climb packages you can choose from. These packages are

- daytime climbs where you can see Greenwich, The Olympic Park, the Canary Wharf, and 360° views of London

- sunset climbs, which give you a romantic view of the city against the backdrop of the setting sun

- twilight climbs, which provides you with a multicolored light experience when you climb the O2

Depending on the package, prices will vary. However, basic tickets to climb the O2 start at £35.

Dinosaur Hunting in Crystal Palace Park

Crystal Palace has plenty of things to do, and it's well-loved for being away from the busy London Streets and tourist attractions. You may not realize that Crystal Palace is also home to dinosaurs. Okay, not like real dinosaurs, but sculptures of them! The dinosaurs are the remains of a former theme park from the Victorian Era and are prime attractions for the palace's garden. So, while enjoying a picnic, coffee, or a stroll through the park, going dinosaur hunting (especially with the littles) is a fun way to spend an afternoon and see how many you can find!

Indulge in Richmond Park

I mentioned Richmond Park earlier but did not get into the full scale of it (aside from mentioning that it is the largest Royal Park). In Richmond Park, you will find that it's a tranquil nature haven. There are trees lining the streets, green parks, and beautiful views of the River Thames. However, visitors love Richmond Park for its open deer park where you can see deer.

Richmond Park offers other fun things to experience, including power kitting,

horseback riding, golfing, hiking, or biking along off-road cycle trails. It's pretty easy to spend an entire day exploring the park, given its expansive size and the various things to do.

Walk Through Streatham Rookery

The Rookery was once a private house and is now home to one of the most gorgeous

formal gardens in the city. There is a collection of ornamental ponds, wildflower beds, planted herbaceous, an Old English Garden, a White Garden, and several ornamental native hedges. This garden is a beautiful space to walk through, especially if you're looking for a light afternoon of adventuring in a quieter space.

Watch an Indie Film at the David Lean Cinema

The David Lean Cinema is in the Croydon Clocktower and offers various indie film screenings six days a week. The cinema has been open since 1995 (minus a brief closure in 2011), making it a rich part of British cinematic history sharing indie-genre films. You can also spend time in their library and museum while in the building and enjoy a specialized drink at their Arts Café Bar.

Find Your Art Style at Peckham Levels

Since Peckham Levels hosts a variety of art spaces among bars and restaurants, this is an excellent spot to view artwork from local artists and shop at other indie businesses.

You likely won't spend an entire day here, but the bar space on the sixth floor has an array of international street food and coffee shops. In addition, you'll find jewelry shops, a tattoo shop, and a hair and wellness center within the varying floors of the building, all supporting the community.

Visit the Museums in Greenwich

Greenwich has an abundance of Royal Museums, all curated to bring you more of this neighborhood's rich history. The Cutty Sark is one of these museums worth climbing aboard to learn more about her time as a tea clipper importing tea from China to the U.K. in addition to the Royal Naval College. However, here are some of the other museums worth checking out:

National Maritime Museum: The National Maritime Museum has over 2 ½ million artifacts to immerse yourself in, including the jacket worn by Admiral Nelson, who was fatally shot at the Battle of Trafalgar.

The Queen's House: The Queen's House offers a fascinating look into one of the critical architectural buildings in the country. This house was the first Classical villa in England and was very different from the Gothic and Tudor styles before this house's construction. This house has an art collection featuring works by Canaletto, Rembrandt, and Gainsborough. You'll also see the iconic portrait of Elizabeth I. Visiting The Queen's House is free, but booking ahead is recommended. They are open between 10 a.m. and 5 p.m. daily.

Ranger's House: Set in a gorgeous Georgian Villa, the Ranger's House is home to over 700 pieces of artwork, from medieval sculptures to elaborate jewelry and Renaissance paintings. Outside, you may notice the house looks familiar, and that is because it was the filming location for the Bridgerton House in Netflix's *Bridgerton*. The hours for Ranger's House are Wednesday to Sunday from 11 a.m. to 4 p.m. Tickets are £12.50 for adults and £7.50 for children between 5 and 17.

Royal Observatory: The Royal Observatory was established in 1675 by Charles II in Greenwich Park to study stars and improve sea navigation. In this museum, you will see the clocks John Harrison invented to determine where longitude was. This is where you can straddle the Meridian line pointing between East and West. The Royal Observatory is open daily between 10 a.m. and 5 p.m. Tickets are £18 for adults, £9 for children, and £12 for students or people under 25.

Find the Spooks at Nunhead Cemetery

Hours of operation:

- **from April 1 to September 30:** 8:30 a.m. to 7 p.m.
- **from October 1 to October 31:** 8:30 a.m. to 5 p.m.
- **from November 1 to February 28:** 8:30 a.m. to 4 p.m.
- **from March 1 to March 31:** 8:30 a.m. to 5 p.m.

Nunhead does not compare to any of the other cemeteries in London—and it's one

of the least well-known ones, which likely adds to its haunting beauty. However, it's more than just a cemetery. It's also partly a wilderness and nature reserve.

Once called the All Saints Cemetery, Nunhead Cemetery was opened in 1840 by the London Cemetery Company. The cemetery was built to relieve other cemeteries in the city that were becoming overcrowded. Like the other cemeteries, it was a place where people could rest peacefully after being buried. The cemetery was a flourishing area for those who passed. Sadly, when a new railway leading to Crystal Palace was installed and, unfortunately, blocked Nunhead's cemetery entrance, the area started to see its end; even after another cemetery entrance was installed, it didn't fix its decline. Eventually, the cemetery became vandalized and was hit during the London Blitz in World War II. The cemetery officially closed its doors in 1969.

As you walk through the paths, you'll find they are crossed with other walkways to lead you to woodland burial plaques. You'll see how Mother Nature took her course, covering some tombstones with vines and branches.

The Nunhead Cemetery also is believed to be home to various ghosts (which shouldn't be shocking given it is a cemetery). Some visitors are sure they have seen a tall, dark person in black clothes emerge from the catacombs and then disappear into the woods. Other visitors have said they've heard the laughter of children playing, sending chills down their spines. Whether or not you believe in ghosts, the Nunhead Cemetery is a beautiful place to go and remember those who have long since passed.

Tour Eltham Palace

Hours of operation: 10 a.m. to 5 p.m. daily (last entrance is at 4:30 p.m.)

Tickets start from £18 per adult and £11 per child.

Eltham Palace was the childhood home of King Henry VIII and is now an Art Deco mansion transformed in the 1930s by Stephen and Virginia Courtauld, two eccentric millionaires.

Walking through the house, you'll get a taste of the Courtaulds' wealthy lifestyle and quirky personality. You can even try on a range of period costumes!

Outside the Eltham estate, walk through the gardens, which blend the 1930s with medieval touches. In addition, walk across the oldest working bridge connecting two banks over a moat and play on a playground inspired by the Courtaulds.

Learn History at Horniman Museum

Museum hours of operation: 10 a.m. to 5:30 p.m. daily

Butterfly House hours of operation: 10:30 a.m. to 4 p.m. daily (last entry is at 3:30 p.m.)

Gardens hours of operation: Monday to Saturday from 7:15 a.m. to 8:30 p.m. and Sundays and Bank Holidays from 8 a.m. to 8:30 p.m.

Immerse yourself in a museum filled with natural history, musical instruments, and anthropology when you visit the Horniman Museum and Gardens. Horniman

House was initially named the Surrey House Museum when it opened in 1890 in the Horniman's house. It moved to a new building in Forest Hill in 1901 under its current name.

When the initial and rebranded museum opened, Frederick Horniman, best known for running his father's tea business, Horniman's Tea, envisioned raising living standards in Britain's society. His goal of opening the museum was to bring the world to the area so people could experience all walks of life while learning about originality and global craftsmanship. It took years of collecting and traveling for the Horniman Museum to have an extensive collection of the artifacts we see today in the galleries.

Of those galleries, here is what to expect in each of them:

The World Gallery: The World Gallery features over 3,000 objects from around the globe, allowing visitors to see other ways of living and learn about various cultures and the people who created them—this was Horniman's vision! In the World Gallery, you can touch Tuareg metalwork, feel the skin from an arctic seal or reindeer, and see the coral reef (digitally) below your feet. In addition, you'll get to smell various herbs used by the Bhutanese ritual healers in the Himalayas and hear First Nations' stories. This gallery is filled with education, and the rich displays will show you a lot about the world while challenging your perspectives.

Natural History Gallery: The Natural History Gallery is a sight to see. This gallery opened in the new museum in 1901, and its design was influenced by Art Nouveau movements and the arts and crafts at the time. The gallery features a display of taxidermy, specimens preserved in fluids, skeletons, and fossils. The taxidermy walrus is one sight that impresses many visitors. The Natural History Gallery will also teach you about his collecting history and how taxidermy flourished in the 19th century.

The Music Gallery: For music lovers, the Music Gallery has 1,300 objects from Horniman's collection of musical instruments, the largest in the U.K. This gallery features short films that connect to the instruments on display, sharing the context and culture of which they are played. In addition to viewing the instruments, you can play with some interactive sound tables that play the sounds of the instruments.

The Gardens: The museum features gardens spanning 16 acres. The Grasslands Garden features plants from the South African grasslands and the North American prairie. The Sunken and Display Gardens were built in 1936 and have botanical displays that connect the indoor and outdoor collections. The Gardeners and Curators have worked closely for decades to reflect various themes and change the plants seasonally.

Aquarium: The aquarium features 15 exhibits of different aquatic environments worldwide, including the British pond to the coral reefs found in Fiji. You will see fish interacting with the reefs, see different types of frogs, and watch the jellyfish move. This aquarium teaches visitors about the animals while seeing them up close and about their life in the wild.

In addition to the various galleries, the Horniman Nature Trail is the oldest in London and was once the original site for the Crystal Palace and South London Junction railway. The railway closed in 1954, and Mother Nature took her course, leaving the area unmanaged until 1973 when the trail opened as a nature walk. The staff at Horniman manages the trail carefully to encourage nature to find its way. If you walk the path, note that it is a sensitive area, and there is a lot of care to keep it open for everyone to enjoy, so don't pick leaves or flowers as they are a critical part of the habitat.

The Horniman Museum has plenty of other things to see around the museum, including a clocktower, conservatory, totem pole, bandstand, mosaic, and Dutch barn.

You do not require a ticket to enter the Horniman Museum or the Gardens. However, if you wish to visit the Aquarium, Butterfly House, and other special exhibitions, the ticket prices will vary between the different areas. You will need to prebook them in advance.

Ticket type	Aquarium	Butterfly House	Special exhibitions
Children	£2.50	£7	As special exhibitions will vary, you will need to check the museum's website for more details and booking information.
Adults	£5	£7	
Family of three (one adult)	£8	£15.50	
Family of four (up to two adults)	£12	£20	
Children under 3	free		

Explore Kew Gardens

Gardens are a botanist's heaven, and Kew Gardens is often high up on their list

with its beautiful colors, thanks to over 50,000 living plants from around the world.

Kew Gardens dates back to 1759 when King George III's mother, Princess Augusta, founded a nine-acre botanic garden within the Kew grounds. Today, it is a place for scientists to research plants and fungi while providing conservation efforts to protect endangered plants.

You will find that Kew Gardens has some beautiful glasshouses housing various plants. In the Palm House, find yourself in an exotic rainforest as if wandering deep into the world's jungles. In the Princess of Wales Conservatory, you'll explore various climates. If you love seeing water lilies, you'll be amazed by their size in the Waterlily House!

Throughout Kew Gardens, you can enjoy other floral displays with over 60,000 plants along the Great Broad Walk Borders and 14,000 trees in the Arboretum (which is exceptionally colorful). If you want a birds-eye view, walking on the Treetop Walkway will take you 59 feet above the gardens to see what they look like from above.

The hours of operation vary based on the time of year, and it is best to visit their website based on when you are visiting to find out the times the Gardens are open. Additionally, the admission prices to Kew Gardens vary based on the season (but it does not apply to children between 4 and 15 years old). Peak season is from February 1 to October 31, and off-peak is from November 1 to January 31. It is best to book the gardens ahead of time to save some money.

Season	Adult	Seniors	Young adult (16 to 29)	Child (4 to 15)
Peak	Advance: £17	Advance: £16	Advance: £8.50	£5
	Standard: £21.50	Standard: £19.50	Standard: £9	
Off-peak	Advance: £12	Advance: £10	Advance: £6	£4
	Standard: £14	Standard: £12	Standard: £6.50	

Children under 4 are free to enter.

If you are visiting with family, the prices are as follows (if you purchase in advance): a family of three (one adult): £24.50 (standard tickets are £28.50), a family of four (up to two adults): £40 (standard tickets are £48)

Tickle your taste buds

South London offers a diverse culinary scene with a mix of traditional British fare and international cuisines that will definitely tickle your taste buds. Here are the best foods to try when you're in South London:

Jerk Chicken: South London, particularly areas like Brixton and Peckham, is

known for its fantastic Caribbean food. Don't miss the opportunity to savor tender, marinated jerk chicken. It's often served with rice and peas, fried plantains, and a flavorful sauce. You can find authentic jerk chicken at local Caribbean eateries and street food stalls.

Nigerian Jollof Rice: South London is home to a vibrant Nigerian community, and you'll find excellent Nigerian restaurants offering dishes like Jollof rice. This

flavorful one-pot rice dish is cooked with tomatoes, peppers, and a blend of spices, creating a delicious and aromatic meal. Pair it with fried plantains and your choice of protein, like chicken or goat.

Portuguese Custard Tarts (Pastéis de Nata): Take a delightful dessert break

with Pastéis de Nata, Portuguese custard tarts that are a true South London favorite. These flaky pastries filled with creamy custard and a hint of cinnamon are available in many local bakeries and cafes.

Ethiopian Injera: Explore the diverse culinary scene of South London by trying

Ethiopian cuisine. Injera, a sourdough flatbread, is a staple. It's used as both a serving platter and an accompaniment to various stews and dishes. Sharing an Ethiopian meal with friends is not only delicious but also a communal dining experience.

Where to Stay in South London

Most people stay central and north of the River Thames when they come to London, but this chapter has shown you that there is much to see and do in the city's south end, too. So, if you want to stay in a different part of town that is still central to various areas of London by public transport, here are some of the top recommendations for accommodations:

Premier Inn London Brixton: As Brixton is an excellent option to stay in since it is around 11 minutes from Central London, the Premier Inn London Brixton is an excellent budget-friendly option, especially if you are traveling with your family. This hotel is near many of Brixton's attractions and the Village Market.

Ibis London Greenwich: Located in Greenwich, the Ibis London Greenwich is 10 minutes from the Royal Observatory, the Greenwich Market, and the Cutty Sark. This budget-friendly hotel is perfect for families and travelers looking for budget-friendly accommodations.

Novotel London Greenwich: The Novotel London Greenwich is conveniently located near public transportation, making it accessible to explore various parts of London. This hotel has spacious rooms, a restaurant serving international foods, and is a 10-minute walk from the Royal Observatory.

Sea Containers London: This luxury hotel in Lambeth is right along the River Thames. Sea Containers London is near the Sea Containers House and seven minutes from the Tate Modern and Shakespeare's Globe Theater by foot. In addition, the hotel has a beautiful riverside restaurant with outdoor seating and a riverside patio and terrace to give you a panoramic view of London.

The Wellington Hotel: The Wellington Hotel is a budget accommodation above a cozy pub. You can easily reach several attractions, including the London Eye, the London Dungeon, and Tate Modern.

The Victoria Inn: The Victoria Inn is a boutique hotel and pub in the center of Peckham. This hotel is near several attractions, including the Horniman Museum and Gardens and Peckham Rye Park. There are 15 rooms available with four different styles, all equipped with a Nespresso machine and Bose Bluetooth sound system to ensure your stay is comfortable and feels like home.

Peckham Rooms Hotel: Peckham Rooms Hotel offers affordable accommodations. It's near public transport to anywhere in London, including the O2 arena, Tower Bridge, and London Bridge.

Hotel du Vin Cannizaro House: Located in Wimbledon, the Hotel du Vin Cannizaro is famous for its wine theme. But it's not just for its delicious wines and food guests stay here for. It's the luxury the hotel provides. This hotel is in an 18th-century building next to the Common, has beautiful grounds for enjoying afternoon tea or other beverages, and is easily accessible to some of South London's popular attractions.

What NOT to Do in South London

It's easy to get caught up in the moment when you're traveling. After all, it's exciting to see the sites and enjoy South London's various experiences. In this section, we will cover some things you should remember while visiting this area (and some things to avoid).

Don't Forget About the Parks

During the summer, most of us want to spend as much time outside as possible (especially when some live in a climate that experiences all four seasons— especially a winter that seems to never end). While trying to cram as much of London as possible into your itinerary is tempting, some days you just need to take a rest day (or afternoon) to enjoy life without trying to go from one place to the next. Visiting one of South London's many parks is an excellent way to do this! You can find a space to picnic or take a stroll. Some of the parks in South London to spend an afternoon in are

- Crystal Palace Park
- Greenwich Park
- Nunhead Cemetery
- Peckham Rye
- Horniman Museum Gardens
- Tooting Commons
- Richmond Park

Don't Forget Croydon Doesn't Have a Tube Station

Croydon is rich in history, especially with it playing an essential role in World War II. However, remember that there isn't a tube station in Croydon. You can get to the neighborhood by the regular train or on a tram.

Don't Skip South London's Culinary Diversity

South London offers a wide range of international cuisines. Don't limit your dining experiences to familiar dishes; be adventurous and try foods from different cultures.

Don't Skip the Local Breweries

South London has a growing craft beer scene. Explore local breweries and enjoy unique, artisanal beers responsibly.

Don't Forget About Queuing at Wimbledon

With Wimbledon back in full swing (no pun intended), you'd be surprised that queuing is just as much a part of the famous event as the actual tennis matches. If you want to go to a game at Wimbledon, the keyword is to line up early. The earlier you're there, the better chance you will get tickets. If you've ever stood out in line waiting to get in somewhere overnight, Wimbledon is no different.

The queue to get day-of tickets for Wimbledon begins in Wimbledon Park. Anyone can join the line early. However, if you arrive late evening, you can only access the lineup at the Wimbledon Park Road Gates. Don't worry. There are stewards to help guide you if you're confused or lost! After you're in the line, you will be given a ticket that will give you an idea of where you are in the queue. Keep this ticket safe because the first 500 people get the best seating picks! Here are some other guidelines to keep in mind:

1. You are officially in line when you have been issued a valid, dated, and numbered Queue Card. You must keep this with you until you've reached the box office. Do not lose it!

2. You cannot transfer the Queue Cards or reserve a place in line for friends coming late.

3. Leaving the line to use the washroom or buy food should not exceed 30 minutes.

4. If you plan to stay in line overnight, you can stay in a tent accommodating a maximum of two people. One person must remain present at all times.

5. If you leave anything unattended, it's gone.

6. You cannot bring a camping stove or barbeque or have a fire in the queue or Wimbledon Park.

7. Be respectful of your fellow queuers. Displaying annoying behavior and playing loud music is not tolerated.

South London might be south of the Thames, but this area has much to see and do. Is it better than North London? That's entirely up to you to decide. However, with the must-do activities like climbing the O2, seeing the beautiful Kew Gardens, and marveling at the world's wonders in the Horniman Museum, you will undoubtedly have a memorable experience. Plus, the energy and excitement are unmatched if you are in London during Wimbledon!

In the next chapter, we'll move into the west side of London (another area where people may say the west is the best). West London is known for its sophisticated neighborhoods, Paddington, and beautiful parklands. Your adventure here will bring you to see some beautiful colors and some international spots that you may not think you would see!

Chapter 8:

West London—Dos and Don'ts

T raditionally speaking, West London is the home of the rich and famous of the city, making it well-known for its charm and sophistication. However, it's a very diverse area, stretching from Marylebone (pronounced meh-ruh-luh-bone) to Acton, with more things to see and do than most people realize.

If you seek urban chic, the West end along Tottenham Court Road, Bond, and Regent Streets are the places to go, where you will find prime shopping and unique boutiques to meet your fancy. In Soho, there are plenty of music venues, bars, and theaters for a fun night out, proving that the West End runs a mile a minute without ever slowing down. However, if it's calmness you seek, the urban area of Marylebone offers that quietness. Plenty of period homes and other boutiques, complete with a farmer's market, provide a chill vibe in this area.

On the corner of the west side is a suburban paradise where West London opened the first garden suburb in the world. The streets are wide, with picturesque homes winding through the various green spaces. This area is rustic but still has public transport nearby to take you to Central London, among other areas.

Lastly, West London should also be experienced simply for their vibrant culture. Several neighborhoods, including Notting Hill and Kensington, offer a mix of quiet streets, walks along the river, and cultural opportunities.

What to DO in West London

Having painted a picture of London's west end, let's look at some of the things you should do in some of their famous neighborhoods.

Kensington and South Kensington

Away from the bustling streets of Central London lies the neighborhoods of Kensington and South Kensington. As this is one of the wealthiest areas in the world, it should come as no surprise that Kensington and South Kensington have a long history dating back to the 12th century, becoming one of the most desired places to live in the 18th century.

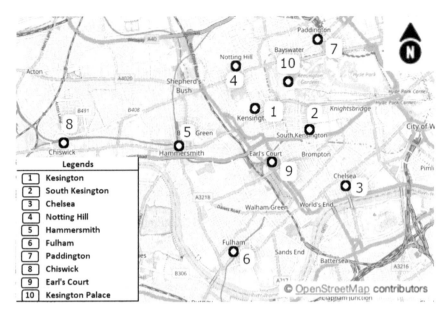

Legends

1	Kesington
2	South Kesington
3	Chelsea
4	Notting Hill
5	Hammersmith
6	Fulham
7	Paddington
8	Chiswick
9	Earl's Court
10	Kesington Palace

With Kensington being a prime location for several famous residents, it has become popular with tourists. Among the gorgeous houses lining the streets, Kensington has three museums, markets, parks, and Kensington Palace. South Kensington has the incredible Natural History Museum, where you can come face-

to-face with a T. rex and feel the power of an earthquake.

While you're in Kensington, visiting some shops on Kensington High Street is a must! There are plenty of shops that suit anyone's needs and interests, including designer and independent shops.

In South Kensington, visit the Victoria and Albert Museum, where you can see and learn about ceramics, furniture, fashion, jewelry, photographs, sculptures, textiles, and paintings from over the past 3,000 years. For a fun-filled family day, go to the Science Museum, where you and your kids can interact with hands-on learning experiences.

Chelsea

Chelsea is home to the football club, Chelsea FC, several swanky restaurants and bars, and the reality show following elite socialites, Made in Chelsea. Like Kensington, Chelsea is undeniably another wealthy neighborhood in West London. Still, aside from the glamourous place that it is, Chelsea has plenty of hidden gems pointing to its origins before its prime.

As you walk through Chelsea, make King's Road one of your places to stroll. King's Road is in the center of Chelsea, and it was once the spot for the fashion world in the 1960s, with several fashion boutiques lining the street. Those shops are long gone and have since been replaced with other shopping options, restaurants, and bars, but it is a hot spot for celebrity sightings, especially when you stop for a bite to eat.

Chelsea has a love affair with flowers, and it's something worth seeing—especially if you're there during the Chelsea Flower Show and Chelsea in Bloom. During these two events in May, Chelsea is decked out with beautiful floral installations. If you're in London outside of the festivals, you can still see flowers! It's a little off King's Road, but the Chelsea Psychic Garden is a hidden gem, with over 5,000 plants that can be used in medicines. This is a beautiful spot to visit if you want to grab a coffee or tea or have breakfast, brunch, or lunch at the café.

Notting Hill

Notting Hill's name is well-known in the 1999 Richard Curtis film of the same name starring Julia Roberts and Hugh Grant. Still, beyond Hollywood, Notting

Hill is beautiful, especially with the homes making for Instagram-worthy shots, thanks to the colorful houses. If you plan to take photos of them, be mindful that these are people's homes, show respect to the homeowners by staying off their property, and don't huddle in large groups to take photos.

However, it's more than just a setting for a movie and Instagram photos. Notting Hill combines chichi cafés, high-end boutiques, and other cool spots. This neighborhood is also family-friendly, with many pubs catering to all ages, making it a great place to eat out on one of your nights in London!

Some other things you must consider doing while in Notting Hill is to go and lose yourself in independent bookstores, especially the Notting Hill Bookstore and Book and Kitchen. In addition, the Museum of Brands is another exciting place to explore because it is dedicated to displaying all sorts of advertising. However, it also takes an in-depth look at how advertising and brands shape our society today and throughout the years.

Finally, in Notting Hill, the Kensal Green Cemetery is a charming area to visit. This beautiful cemetery expands over 72 acres of land and has gorgeous Gothic-style monuments and tombs in the overgrown garden. Several actors, writers, and artisans are buried here, including Maria Graham, one of the world's first travel writers!

Hammersmith

Hammersmith is a borough along the River Thames, giving you beautiful river

views as you stroll along its edge. Along the river is the Upper and Lower Mall containing historical rowing clubs, and the Hammersmith Bridge, a suspension bridge marking the halfway point for the Boat Race held annually between Cambridge and Oxford Universities. Interestingly, this bridge was opened in June 1887 and was the second bridge to cross the River Thames in this spot. A former suspension bridge stood there before but could not support increased road traffic. Its final straw was when a crowd of 12,000 people came to watch the 1870 annual Boat Race. If you look closely, you will see the original foundations on which this bridge stands.

If you are looking for a pint or a bite to eat, step into The Dove. This pub dates back to the 18th century and was the stomping grounds for various famous clientele, including writers Ernest Hemingway, William Morris, and Dylan Thomas.

After you finish your pint and meal, continue walking along the Thames Path, home to some breathtaking Georgian and Regency homes overlooking the river. You'll also find some green spaces that look rural.

When you return to the Hammersmith Bridge, you may be tempted to cross it, and it's worth it if you do, as the WWT London Wetland Center is on the other side. This 100-acre nature reserve was once an industrial area for Victorian reservoirs. The space was converted into the wetland center that opened in 2000 and has since attracted various birds—some of which have never been seen elsewhere in London.

If you're looking for other quiet areas to spend your time, take the time to escape to Ravenscourt Park. There you will find a walled garden that feels like a secret garden, a tree-lined pond, and a couple of cafés.

Fulham

Sandwiched between Chelsea and Hammersmith, Fulham is one of the most

untouched areas by tourists because its previous fame was being a place for residents, chain restaurants, and sports clubs. However, Fulham has flourished and grown over the years with plenty of things to see and do, including exploring some of its medieval traits.

Along the Thames Path is one of London's most important botanical gardens and the former home to 133 London bishops at the Fulham Palace. In 1601, Queen Elizabeth I was a guest of honor during a banquet. The palace's garden covers 13 acres with colorful flowers, trees, Britain's oldest holm oak.

While in Fulham, you may also stroll through the Brompton Cemetery, another cemetery that is part of the "magnificent seven." You may be wondering why you want to continue walking through cemeteries because they do have a bit of a creep factor built into them. However, although it is somewhat overgrown, it is the U.K.'s sole Crown Cemetery and is the final resting place for famous people, including

- Dr. Benjamin Golding, founder of Charing Cross Hospital

- Emmeline Pankhurst, the British activist who organized the suffragette movement

- Sir Henry Cole, an English Public Servant, art patron, and a significant influencer behind the Great Exhibition

For shopping opportunities in Fulham, head to Jordan Place on Fulham Broadway to peruse through some unique shops. At the North End Road Market (open Monday through Saturday), you'll find several bargains and fresh fruits, vegetables, and hot meals.

Paddington

Paddington is famous for the marmalade-loving bear. However, in 1928, it was at

St. Mary's Hospital where Alexander Fleming revolutionized medicine by discovering penicillin that the neighborhood of Paddington received its original fame. St. Mary's Hospital is also where Prince Harry, Prince William, Prince George, and Princess Charlotte were born. Whether you come to Paddington to get a little closer to the Royals or to find the famous bear, there are plenty of historical touches among the modern attractions for any age.

One of the fun activities you should definitely do (whether or not you are in London with Kids) is to follow the Pawprint Trail, which will take you through some of London's best landmarks. These junctures are connected to Paddington Bear, and all stops will contain stories and fun facts about the bear's journey.

Merchant Square is another fun place to head, especially during summer, to try out the water maze. The goal is simple: find your way through the maze without getting wet!

For unique dining experiences, you can find a taste of Australia in Paddington. Climb aboard the Darcie and May Green Floating Restaurant and Bar! This restaurant offers an unforgettable evening with Australian-inspired dishes for brunch, lunch, and dinner.

After your meal, take the time to check out some of Paddington's cool Basin Bridges. There are five in total along the canal, each sharing unique views of London, lush green parks, Victorian terraces, and more.

Lastly, if you didn't notice this in Paddington Station or want to find some other historical monuments in the area, on Platform 1 is the statue of The Unknown Soldier. This powerful statue is a reminder of the many soldiers who fought and lost their lives in the country during World War I (and in the wars that followed), encapsulating the sacrifices and courage shown during times of conflict.

Chiswick

Located just 30 minutes to an hour outside Central London is Chiswick, a neighborhood with a bit of village and city in its borough. Most residents describe

this rustic area as a leafy haven, and it happens to be the home of several known actors, including Colin Firth, Hugh Grant, and David Tennant.

People love to come to Chiswick primarily for its beauty, especially at Chiswick House and Gardens. This building served as an asylum between 1892 and 1928. Outside the house is a pleasant green space and a conservatory free for visitors to walk through. However, if you want to visit the house, there is a fee to get in.

Chiswick has markets that happen every Sunday if pursuing these is something of interest to you. They are lively and have different themes each week, including

- the Chiswick Flower Market, which happens every first Sunday of the month

- the Chiswick Antiques and Vintage Market, which happens every second Sunday of the month

- the Chiswick Cheese Market, which happens every third Sunday of the month

- the Food Market Chiswick, which happens every Sunday morning

Earl's Court

Before Earl's Court became what it is today, it was once vast farmland until the Metropolitan District Railway expanded out that way. After World War II ended, Earl's Court saw an increase in residents from Poland, Australia, and New Zealand.

As you walk through Earl's Court, you will see beautiful neighborhoods and houses lining the streets surrounded by green spaces. There are several townhomes available to rent for your vacation, too. However, while walking through the various streets in Earl's Court, it's worth going to 153 Cromwell Road, where Alfred Hitchcock lived. There isn't a museum, and the house is privately owned, but it's a neat place to stop and see where one of the greatest horror-genre directors resided. Another famous house to stop by is the Garden Lodge, where Queen's leading man, Freddie Mercury, lived. This house is not open to the public, and a brick wall surrounds it. It's still a popular place to take a selfie.

England is well known for their ales and ciders, so you may not think to go to a winery—but they do exist! London Cru makes some delicious wines with grapes and fruit grown throughout Europe's vineyards. London Cru offers wine tastings and tours so you can learn how wine is made in a city setting.

London's red telephone booths are a staple along the streets of London—the blue police ones? Not so much. Though the need for blue police boxes has been phased out over the years, one remains outside the Earl's Court Tube Station. It does still work, so don't use it unless you must. However, given its fame for being the TARDIS in the popular science fiction show *Doctor Who*, it makes for a fun selfie (even though you won't be able to use it to travel through space or time and it's definitely *not* bigger on the inside).

What to Enjoy in West London

West London has plenty of things you must do in the area, from following Paddington Bear's journey through London to seeing where Freddie Mercury and Alfred Hitchcock lived. But aside from the must-do, here are some things you should enjoy and experience in West London.

Visit Kensington Palace

Hours of operation:

- Monday and Tuesday: Crown Couture tours only

- Wednesday to Sunday: 10 a.m. to 6 p.m. (last entry is at 5 p.m.)

Step into the history of the Royals in Kensington Palace, the birthplace of Queen Victoria and the former residence of the Duke and Duchess of Cambridge (they have now moved to Adelaide Cottage).

Kensington Palace will take you through 300 years of history surrounding the Royal family as you can stroll through the halls, view the state apartments filled with paintings and sculptures, and walk through the gardens. There are also reminders of Princess Diana's life, including an official memorial. This is a wonderful way to spend an afternoon if you want to experience living a Royal life. Here are the ticket prices for Kensington Palace:

Ticket type	Price
Adults	£25.40
Children (5 to 15)	£12.70
Seniors (65 and up) and visitors with a disability	£20.30

Children under 5 and carers for disabled visitors are free.

Shop at Portobello Road Market

Notting Hill's Portobello Road is a place to go if you're looking to shop in a diverse  group of stores. However, on Saturdays, the road transforms into a market with lively vendors selling antiques, street food, vintage clothing, and much more.

This market can sometimes feel crowded due to other tourists, but it is one of the best markets in London and worth the trip, even for a couple of hours. Going earlier in the day is better if you want to beat the crowds. The market runs from 7 a.m. to 7 p.m.

Watch a Rugby Match at Twickenham Stadium

The grand Twickenham Stadium is the official home of England rugby, making it one of the most famous attractions, especially for rugby fans. Over 80,000 spectators gather and yell their heads off during the game, making it an exciting event in London.

Even if Rugby is not your thing (or you will not be in West London when a game is happening), you should consider taking a tour of Twickenham. On the tour, you will learn about the stadium's history dating back to 1907 and the first game held there. On the tour, you'll also see the changing rooms, pitch-side, and more. The tour of the stadium takes 90 minutes. Here are the dates and times:

- from Tuesday to Friday at 10:30 a.m., 12:30 p.m., and 2:30 p.m.

- Saturdays at 10:30 a.m., 12 p.m., 1 p.m., and 2:30 p.m.

- Sundays at 11:30 a.m., 1 p.m., and 2:30 p.m.

The pricing for the tours is as follows:

Ticket type	Price
Adults	£22.75
Children (5 to 15)	£12.70
Young adults (16 and up)	£22.95
Seniors (65 and up) and visitors with a disability	£22.95

Children under 5 (three per one adult) and carers for disabled visitors are free.

See a Performance at the Royal Albert Hall

The Royal Albert Hall is one of the most historic buildings in Britain. Completed in 1871 with beautiful archways, pillars, and tiers of seating topped with an impressive dome.

The Royal Albert Hall has an array of shows to cater to any interest, from watching an orchestra to stand-up comedy.

In addition to catching a performance at the Royal Albert Hall, touring it is another must-do experience. These tours will take you through a classical tour of the building, or you can take a behind-the-scenes tour otherwise off-limits to the public. There are plenty of tour options, so visiting the website of the Royal Albert Hall will help guide you on which tour is the best option for you.

See Modern Art at the Saatchi Gallery

Hours of operation: Monday to Sunday from 10 a.m. to 6 p.m.

The Saatchi Gallery has been a frontrunner in contemporary art since 1985. Showcasing the works of emerging artists, the Saatchi Gallery has displayed some of the biggest names in art history, such as Andy Warhol. If you love Andy Warhol, you can catch some of his works on permanent display here while seeing the works of other artists. This gallery is free to visit, but donations are welcomed.

Spend Time in the Kyoto Garden

As you will see throughout London, plenty of green spaces offer beautiful views, but Kyoto Garden is something else.

Kyoto Garden occupies a part of Holland Park and has been manicured to replicate a Japanese garden. As you stroll through the winding paths, you will see perfectly cut lawns, stone lanterns, waterfalls, Japanese maple trees, and shrubs. You may even come across a couple of peacocks. This garden is the definition of an oasis and one place worth spending some time in to get away from the hustle and bustle of West London. Holland Park opens daily at 7:30 a.m. and closes half an hour before dusk.

Wander Through Museum Mile

West London has 13 museums within a square mile of one another, but if you are pressed for time, which ones should you go to? Let's take a look at a few options.

The Charles Dickens Museum

Famous for writing *A Christmas Carol, Oliver Twist,* and *A Tale of Two Cities*, at the Charles Dickens Museum, you can step into the author's home and browse his collection of pictures, first editions, furniture, and much more in the restored bedroom. This is a must for people who appreciate literature. The museum is open from Wednesday to Sunday between 10 a.m. and 5 p.m. The admission prices are as follows:

- adults: £12.50

- seniors (60 and up) and disabled visitors: £10.50

- children (6 to 16 years old): £7.50

Children under 6 are free.

Science Museum

Enter the world of science with over seven floors of fun, educational exhibits at the Science Museum. There are several interactive galleries to challenge your mind, exhibits exploring space, and much more. You can visit this museum between 10 a.m. and 6 p.m. daily; tickets are free but must be prebooked.

The Cartoon Museum

Hours of operation: Tuesday, Wednesday, Friday, and Sunday: 10:30 a.m. to 5:30 p.m., Thursday: 10:30 a.m. to 8 p.m., Closed on Mondays

Looking for something that brings your inner child out to play? The Cartoon Museum has over 6,000 original comics and cartoons on display, with an extensive library filled with books and comics. You'll see works of satire, advertisements, and colorful graphics throughout the museum—you may even find some of your favorites! This is the museum where you are encouraged to laugh!

To enter the cartoon museum, it is £9.50 for adults, £6 for adults over 60, and free for visitors under 18 or if you have a London Pass.

Natural History Museum

Probably one of the most beautiful museums in London, the Natural History Museum is famous for its collection of 70 million dinosaur skeletons, fossils, and much more. There is so much to do for solo travelers, adults, and children that this is one museum you should plan to spend the day in. This museum is open daily from 10 a.m. to 5:50 p.m. (the last entry is at 5:30 p.m.). Tickets are free for all visitors, but book them in advance!

Other museums within museum mile that are worth checking out and that we have already covered in this book include The British Library and the London Transport Museum

Go Through Hampton Court Palace's Maze

Hampton Court Palace is the home of Henry VIII and is rich in history. But aside from touring the Great Hall and Tudor kitchens, the garden has a fun maze. It's the oldest hedge maze in Britain, constructed in 1700 by William III. Planning to walk through the maze requires buying a ticket into the palace, but at least you'll get to learn plenty of things inside before retreating outside to play. Tickets are £26.30 for adults and £13.10 for children. There are several opening times based on the season, so it's best to check out their website when you go to prebook your tickets to find out what the hours are based on your travels to London.

Learn About Designs at the Design Museum

Going to a museum focused on design may not be a place that immediately comes to mind, especially when there are plenty of other museums to explore in London. However, at the Design Museum, you will see all the designs that helped shape London's culture. This museum has several items from around the world, including fashion, architecture, engineering, and technology. It's an interesting museum because it gives visitors the perspective of how design is cultivated between the designer and user.

The Design Museum is free to enter, and the hours of operation are from 10 a.m. to 5 p.m., Mondays to Thursdays, and 10 a.m. to 6 p.m. on Fridays to Sundays.

Local cuisine to savor

West London offers a diverse culinary landscape, ranging from traditional British dishes to international cuisine. Here are the best foods to try when you're in West London:

Portobello Road Market Street Food: Head to Notting Hill's Portobello Road  Market for a vibrant street food experience. Sample gourmet burgers, Caribbean jerk chicken, Spanish paella, and a variety of international dishes from the diverse range of stalls lining the market.

Roast Duck in Chinatown: Explore the bustling streets of London's Chinatown  in Soho, located in West London. Try succulent roast duck or crispy duck with pancakes at one of the authentic Chinese restaurants in the area. Pair it with other dim sum and Chinese specialties.

Kensington High Street Dining: Kensington offers a range of upscale dining options. Explore the area's fine dining restaurants and try dishes like British beef Wellington, gourmet seafood, and international cuisine prepared by renowned chefs.

Where to Stay in West London

There are plenty of reasons why you should stay in West London—one being that you'll be close to several attractions in and around West London, particularly Central London. Plus, having a quieter area makes for a pleasant and quiet evening for some downtime. As far as accommodations go, most of it is in the mid-to-luxurious range, but there are a few budget-friendly options. Here are some places to consider:

The Resident Kensington: Although the Resident Kensington is a budget-friendly accommodation, you would be surprised by the luxury this hotel offers. The rooms in the Resident Kensington have a kitchenette and Nespresso machine and provide sustainable toiletries. That's just the rooms, though. This hotel is also within steps of Central London, making it an excellent option for walking to most landmarks.

The Portobello Hotel: The Portobello Hotel is a popular option in West London and is the place to stay if you want to be close to celebrities who also love this accommodation. The 21 hotel rooms are split between two converted Neoclassical mansions reflecting the beauty and class of Notting Hill. You'll be steps away from the Portobello Road Market, among other attractions in this area.

The Ampersand Hotel: This pleasant and luxurious boutique hotel will have you feeling like you have a new home in Southwest London. Each room in the Ampersand Hotel has a different style with Victorian furnishings. Guests love this hotel for its beautiful foyer, delicious on-site Mediterranean restaurant, and proximity to the tube, the Natural History Museum, and Hyde Park.

Queen's Gate: The Queen's Gate is a fantastic hotel in West London. The rooms are beautifully furnished with bold wallpaper and a nod to some famous people who have lived in this part of London, including Winston Churchill. The hotel is near Hyde Park, with several museums and shopping at your feet.

Room2 Chiswick: Offering an eco-friendly environment, room2 Chiswick is a trendy accommodation with handmade furniture to furnish the rooms, and they have beautiful, warehouse-type windows to allow plenty of daylight. All rooms have a kitchenette. However, a continental breakfast is offered daily in their restaurant. In addition to a comfortable, eco-friendly stay, room 2 Chiswick has a full gym with Peloton bikes for your workout needs.

The Boathouse: Located in Paddington, The Boathouse is where a super yacht feel and accommodation meet in this one-room boat accommodation. Furnished with a rustic vibe, The Boathouse has one double cabin with a sofa bed, a beautiful bathroom, and a skylight. Guests have the entire boat to themselves, and if you need or want to use a bicycle, they are available for no additional cost.

Hotel 55: If you are traveling to London for business (as well as pleasure), Hotel 55 is one of the favorite accommodation options for work and play. Located next to Kew Gardens, each room features a botanical theme with contemporary artwork. You have the option of rooms ranging from small, cozy spaces to an expansive studio with a private terrace filled with plants. In addition, Hotel 55 offers a delicious, on-site Japanese restaurant with authentic dishes.

Brook Green Hotel: Above a British pub on Shepherd's Bush Road in Hammersmith, the Brook Green Hotel has 17 beautiful rooms in various styles and sizes to meet your traveling needs. Guests can enjoy a traditional English breakfast each morning and, in the evening, unwind with cozy meals inside the pub with open fires, leather couches, and a garden terrace.

What NOT to Do in West London

West London will have plenty of things to do and see. But while there, remember your surroundings when visiting and walking around to keep yourself safe, be patient and courteous while visiting the palaces, and don't forget to prebook your tickets for some of the attractions. Here are other things to avoid or consider when planning a day or two in West London.

Don't Forget West London Is Expensive

Staying in West London is convenient given that it's close to many of the major attractions around London. Some accommodation prices have to do with location. While there are budget-friendly options available in West London, if you're sticking to a tight budget, you may want to consider staying elsewhere.

Don't Miss Having a Picnic in a West London Park

Being in West London will tempt you to visit all the major attractions. But that can make for an exhausting day! So, depending on how long you plan to be in West London, maybe it's a good idea to break up your day and have a picnic in one of the parks to rest for a few hours and eat. Some of the best parks to enjoy a scenic picnic in West London include St. James' Park, Richmond Park, Kensington Palace Gardens and Holland Park

Don't Skip Local Bookstores

West London has charming independent bookshops. Support local businesses by exploring these bookstores and enjoying the literary culture.

Don't Forget to Explore Local Galleries

West London is home to many art galleries, including the Saatchi Gallery and the Serpentine Galleries. Enjoy the art but follow gallery rules and exhibit etiquette.

West London's big and beautiful area has plenty of things to see and do, so deciding where you want to go and what you must see can feel overwhelming. However, in this chapter, you were given several ideas of places you should consider seeing and doing while in West London as this place is undeniably one of the prettiest parts of the city, from spending a few hours in Kyoto Garden or Kew Garden to wandering the grounds in Kensington Palace.

This is all for London and what you should see and do, but you don't need to limit yourself to staying within London as there are other adventures on day trips outside the capital city.

Chapter 9:

Day Trips from London

People don't take trips—trips take people. –John Steinbeck

O utside of the bustling streets of London comes several beautiful country and seaside towns, all with their charm, mystery, and rich history. This bonus chapter outlines some things you should do on a day trip outside London to get a different view of England.

Stonehenge

About 2 hours southwest of Central London in Salisbury is the greatest mystery in England: Stonehenge. What was the purpose of these rocks in this formation?

It is arguably one of the world's iconic landmarks in archaeology. The circle of stones created some 4,600 years ago leaves visitors in awe—not just for the way it was constructed but for the fact that there is no written record of the ancient Britons who built it.

What we do know is that Stonehenge was built in several phases. The first phase began in 3000 B.C.E. with a circular earthwork dug with antlers to create an inner and outer bank. Archeologists believe Stonehenge was the final resting place for about 150 cremation burials from 3000 to 2300 B.C.E. based on excavations revealing human bones. This revelation determined Stonehenge to be the largest burial site in Britain. However, more interesting is that the round pits (Aubrey holes) were not believed to be used for graves but as part of a mysterious religious ceremony.

In the second stage of Stonehenge (2150 B.C.E.), 82 bluestones were brought to the site. How they got there is another mysterious piece of Stonehenge. Remember, these stones do not weigh anything like a small pebble on the beach. They weigh between 2 and 5 tons! Most archeologists think humans moved the bluestones over water and land, but others wonder if glaciers helped move the gigantic stones! Either way, the journey to get the rocks there was around 240 miles.

When the bluestones arrived at the site, they were set up in the center to create an incomplete double circle.

In the third stage of creating Stonehenge (2000 B.C.E.), the Sarsen stones arrived from the Marlborough Downs, about 25 miles north of Stonehenge near Avebury in north Wiltshire. Like the bluestones, the Sarsen stones were not light. They weigh up to 55 tons, making transporting them via water impossible. The only way humans would have been able to move them was by rollers and ropes—500 men to heave the monster stone and another 100 to lay the rollers in front of the stone as it moved. Once they arrived at the site, the rocks were arranged to create the outer circle of Stonehenge.

The final stage of creating Stonehenge came to life in 1500 B.C.E. when the bluestones were moved around to create the horseshoe within the circle, thus making the iconic monument we see today.

Getting to Stonehenge

By Train

There are a few options available for getting to Stonehenge from London. Taking the train is one of the best options. You will need to catch the train at London Waterloo Station. The direct ride is around an hour and 25 minutes in both directions. Your other train station option is to catch a train at the Clapham Junction in the Clapham neighborhood opposite Chelsea.

When you reach Salisbury, you must catch a tour bus or a taxi to get to Stonehenge. The tour bus will take around 25 minutes, but you will get other information and see other sites this way. It's also hard to determine how much a cab might cost, making the tour bus more cost-efficient.

By National Express Coach

If you don't want to catch the train, you can arrange to get to Stonehenge from London by taking a National Express Coach. It will take longer (around three hours and 15 minutes) and won't take you directly to the rock formation. You must change buses or take a taxi when you get to Salisbury.

By Car

Renting a car is another good option (and will be quicker than taking public transportation). You can park near Stonehenge at a parking lot operated by English Heritage. You must pay for parking if you have not prebooked your ticket or purchased an Overseas Visitor Pass, which gives you access to many of England's historical attractions.

One thing to remember when renting a car is to be mindful of your gas and car rental budget. It can also be tricky to navigate, especially with Central London's congestion charge.

Taking an Organized Tour

An organized tour is another way to get to Stonehenge. However, be prepared for a full day as these tours will take you to other historical landmarks, including Windsor Castle, Bath, West Country, and other areas, depending on which tour you go with. If you go with this option, entry fees are covered for most sites, which is a bonus, and you'll see other parts of England along the way.

Whichever way you choose to get to Stonehenge, it is one monument you should not miss. Rocks are neat when we see them in our national parks, but to see something that was physically created thousands of years ago with no understanding as to why is impossible to put into words. It's mysterious, beautiful, breathtaking, and amazing to see in person.

Stonehenge Tickets and Operating Hours

Stonehenge is open daily from 9:30 a.m. to 7 p.m. The hours are subject to change on the Solstices. You can access the site up to two hours before closing. Double-check the opening schedule if something has changed on their website.

The ticket prices listed below are subject to change based on the season and day of the week you plan to go to Stonehenge.

Ticket type	Price
Adult	£20.90
Child (5 to 17)	£12.70
Seniors (65 and up)	£18.10
Family (two adults and up to three children)	£54.50
Family (one adult and up to three children)	£33.60

What NOT to Do at Stonehenge

When you get to Stonehenge, there are a few things to be mindful of when you are there to ensure a pleasurable experience when you visit this iconic landmark.

Don't Expect to Walk Through the Stones

When you get to Stonehenge, you will notice roped fences line the pathway up to and in front of the monument. Crossing the roped fence to walk through the stones and take a selfie within them is prohibited, and you'll be kicked out. Stay on the other side of the fence, admire the stones from afar, and find other creative ways to take a selfie with them in the background.

Don't Bring Drones

Flying drones over Stonehenge is prohibited as drones can disrupt the experience for other visitors and may pose safety risks.

Don't Bring Pets

Pets are not allowed within the Stonehenge monument area. Leave your furry friends at home or arrange for pet care while you visit.

Don't Rush Through the Visitor Center

It'll be tempting to rush through the visitor center at Stonehenge, but by doing so, you'll miss out on plenty of learning opportunities, including learning more about how it was built.

Windsor

Before Windsor Castle towered over the heart of the town, Windsor's origins began its life as a Saxon village, with the Saxons inhabiting the area due to its positioning beside the river. The town was home to up to 150 people until William the Conqueror, the first Norman King, moved in and took the land as his own, creating the iconic Windsor Castle in the year 1070. When the castle was built, timber was used to construct the building. However, when William's grandson Henry II converted the castle into a palace, he replaced the timber with stones and added

apartments. Windsor's transformation was only beginning, though.

When King Edward III reigned, he transformed Windsor Castle from a palace to a military fortification. It was a hefty price to do this, too—a whopping £50,000 for the conversion!

Throughout its years, Windsor Palace has remained a staple to the Royal Family. Queen Victoria spent most of her time there, and when King George VI took the throne after his brother Edward VIII abdicated it, he also lived at a Royal Lodge in Windsor Great Park. As such, Windsor Castle became a special place for King George VI's daughters, Princess Elizabeth and Princess Margaret. This castle remained a special place to Elizabeth, who became the longest-reigning Queen the world has ever seen.

St. George's Chapel at Windsor Castle is another special place for the monarchy. It wasn't added to the palace until 1475, with its construction concluding in 1528. The chapel is of high importance in the royal family as it serves as the final resting place for the Queen, Prince Philip, and the successors who came before Queen Elizabeth II.

Visiting Windsor Castle

When you visit Windsor Castle, you will see the State Apartments, where some monarchies reside at this grand palace. In addition, you can see the ceremonial rooms still used today, historical rooms, Queen Mary's Dollhouse, and St. George's Chapel. Group tours are available for groups of 15 or more. However, you can also take a self-guided tour of Windsor Castle using their free multimedia tour.

If you missed the Changing of the Guard at Buckingham Palace, you can try again at Windsor Castle! The times are the same as Buckingham Palace (weather permitting).

Windsor Castle Tickets and Operating Hours

Windsor Castle is open from Thursday through Sunday. The operating hours are as follows:

- **March 1 to October 31:** 10 a.m. to 5:15 p.m. (last admission time is at 4 p.m.)

- **November 1 to February 28:** 10 a.m. to 4:15 p.m. (last admission time is at 3 p.m.)

As Windsor Castle is a working royal palace, these times and dates are subject to change, and the castle or state apartments may need to close with little notice. Always check their website for details on upcoming closures to avoid disappointment.

Ticket type	Advance tickets	On the day
Adult	£28	£30
Young Adults (18 to 24)	£18	£19.50
Children (5 to 17) and visitors with a disability	£15.50	£16.50

Children under 5 are free, but a ticket must still be booked for them.

St. George's Chapel Tickets and Hours of Operation

Your ticket to Windsor Castle includes St. George's Chapel. However, you can only go to the chapel on Mondays, Thursdays, Fridays, and Saturdays, and access may be limited after 2:30 p.m. You can go for free on Sundays if you want to attend a service; no ticket is required. If you plan to attend a service, you must be at the King Henry VIII gate no later than 15 minutes before the service begins.

Getting to Windsor

Seeing as Windsor Castle is a top tourist attraction outside of London, it can take longer to get there than anticipated (if you take the bus or drive). However, the beauty of traveling, even if it's not quick, is seeing the journey along the route.

By Train

Taking the train from anywhere to Windsor is one of the most direct and efficient ways to get to your destination. Windsor is 23 miles from London, so it's not a long commute (but this also depends on where your departure point is).

Windsor is served by the Great Western Railway (from Paddington Station) and South Western Railway (from London Waterloo Station), offering frequent services between the two. The castle is a short walk from the station, no matter which train you choose.

By Steam Train

To travel by steam train is a dream of many, so if you're going to be in London between June and September, why not choose this mode of transportation to get to Windsor Castle? The Royal Windsor Steam Express is a one-way trip to Windsor Castle. In some ways, it'll be like riding the train to Hogwarts (not quite, but close enough). The steam train departs from London Waterloo Station on Tuesdays and is a classic way to travel to Windsor.

By Bus

The bus is certainly not the fastest way to get to Windsor, but it does give you an outlook of other towns as you drive out to the area. The bus is an excellent option for budgets as well. The Transport for London's Green Line buses serve Windsor and depart from the London Victoria Station. It takes 90 minutes to reach Windsor, but you'll see other spots along the way.

By an Organized Tour

The preferred option for getting to Windsor Castle and the surrounding area is an organized tour. It will make for a longer day, so it may not be the best option if you are on a tight schedule. However, if you have a day to spare, organized tour buses will take you to Windsor Castle, where you will have a guided tour of the palace, see the Royal tombs, and see the Changing of the Guard ceremony, and then take you to other spots, such as Stonehenge and Cambridge.

By Car

Lastly, if you're brave enough to drive in England, you can take a car to get to Windsor. However, if you are going to take a vehicle, the same guidelines apply from earlier in the chapter.

Other Things to Do in Windsor

While Windsor Castle is the main attraction and reason people travel to Windsor, there are other things worth exploring and experiencing while you are there.

Walk Along The Long Walk

Leading up to the front of Windsor Castle is a three-mile avenue called The Long

Walk. The avenue is lined with beautiful trees on either side and as you walk, you're likely to come across one of the many red deer in the park. In addition, taking a stroll through one or all three of the gardens nearby is a must. These gardens are The Savill Garden, The Valley Garden, and Virginia Water. The Long Walk is also a great picnic spot.

Take a Boat Tour

Another way to admire Windsor Castle is by riding along the Thames on a French Brothers Boat Trip. It's a 40-minute round trip that brings you upstream to Boveney Lock. Along the route, you will see Windsor Castle, Eton College (where Prince Harry and William went), Mill House, Windsor Racecourse, and Brocas Meadows. Double-check their website for departure times, as the hours vary based on the season.

Take a Bike Tour

If you're up for a bike ride around Windsor, joining a small bike tour is an excellent and personal way to see Windsor. The bike tour will take you through some of Windsor's lovely scenery and other highlights of the Thames Valley. You will see more sights of Windsor on the bicycle tour in less time (plus you'll get a little exercise).

Stroll Through Alexandra Gardens

Alexandra Gardens is a lovely park across from the Thames. These gardens are a beautiful place to picnic and hang out on the grass. If you are in Windsor during the winter months, you can enjoy ice skating in the rink.

Whatever you decide to do in Windsor, you will have a great time being in the area and exploring the charming town while walking the same streets as the monarchy.

What NOT to Do in Windsor

When you head to Windsor, the castle is undoubtedly one of the spots you'll be checking out. However, there are other things to do in this quaint town, so remember these things so you don't miss out on what is happening in Windsor!

Don't Forget the Security Checks at Windsor Castle

As Windsor is the home of His Majesty The King and a working palace, it should be no surprise that there are thorough security checks before you can tour the building. The security check is similar to going through an airport, so remove metal objects from your pockets before walking through the security arch.

Additionally, you cannot bring large bags or heavy luggage to Windsor Castle. However, you can carry small handbags or backpacks.

Don't Forget to Check the Racing Calendar

The Royal Windsor Racecourse and Ascot are near Windsor's town center, and aside from hosting races, these courses host other fun events, including outdoor movie nights. Depending on when you intend to go to Windsor, double-check the calendar to see what is happening at the Royal Windsor Racecourse or Ascot.

Don't engage with the Guard

If you encounter a guard on duty, do not touch, interact with, or attempt to distract them. They are on duty and should be respected.

Don't Expect to Experience St. George's Chapel on Sundays

St. George's Chapel is an example of the finest Gothic architecture in England and is most famous for being the site of Prince Harry and Meghan Markle's Royal Wedding. If you intend to go to St. George's Chapel, don't expect to experience it on a Sunday, as the chapel is closed to the public.

Cambridge

Cambridge is home to the world's oldest and most prestigious school, Cambridge University, which opened in 1209. While this town has been around for centuries, so much and yet so little is known about its history. It might have to do with the fact that it was established as its town until 1951, which may explain why Google gives you information on Cambridge in Ontario, Canada first, instead of the U.K. town. Even so, Cambridge is a typical English town with its flare and characteristics, and human settlement began way back in ancient Roman times.

Cambridge is a prime example of being a quintessential town in England. Yes, the university has something to do with it, but it also has to do with the culture. Many buildings you will see in Cambridge date back hundreds of years. Whether you wander the campuses or green spaces in Cambridge or go to admire the college buildings, you will find yourself deeply immersed in their culture.

As for their college universities, Cambridge is home to 31 of them. Famous scientists like Sir Issac Newton, Charles Darwin, and Stephen Hawking are alumni of Cambridge University, among stars like Emma Thompson and Tom Hiddleston. Cambridge University has also seen an impressive total of 89 Nobel Prizes from its former students through the six disciplines! It's no wonder that many scholars argue this school is the best.

If you are only spending 24 hours in Cambridge, here are some of the things you must do and see while here:

- **Have brunch at Fitzbillies:** This restaurant has been around since 1921 and serves the best buns in England.

- **Wonder around the Fitzwilliam Museum:** This small museum and art gallery has a significant collection of work by artists such as Rembrandt and Munch.

- **Take a bike tour on a vintage bike:** Strolling around the campuses is one way to see the sights, but a bike is better (and faster). Bike tours are available in Cambridge, and you'll see all the colleges' significant areas in two-and-a-half hours.

- **Visit Cambridge University's botanical gardens:** Cambridge University's botanical gardens house over 8,000 plants from around the world on 40 acres. There are plenty of plants and flowers to see all year round, even in the winter!

- **Shop along Mill Road:** Mill Road has a collection of bookshops, thrift stores, indie cafés, and pubs. This is a fun street to wander through, especially if live music is playing at a coffee shop or pub.

- **Listen to Evensong at King's College Chapel:** Regardless of your beliefs, you will always get goosebumps when you hear a choir singing in a church, especially the choir at King's College Chapel. This group sings various hymns, and the sound is hauntingly beautiful.

- **Punt along the River Cam:** Punting along the River Cam is popular in Cambridge. It lets you see Cambridge University and other parts of the town from the river. It's a challenge to master initially, but you'll be a pro at it in no time!

- **Go to The Eagle for a pint:** The Eagle is a 16th-century pub with plenty of history. There is graffiti left over from World War II airmen who were a part of the RAF bar, which you can see as you enjoy your pint. In addition, this pub is where molecular biologists Francis Crick and James Watson announced their discovery of a DNA double helix in 1953.

- **See Cambridge's view from Great St. Mary's Church:** Great St. Mary's Church has an excellent view of Cambridge. It's a small fee to climb the spiral staircase to the top, but you get to see the town from a different perspective when you get there. It's a beautiful view and worth the climb!

Getting to Cambridge

Being only 64 miles out of London, traveling to Cambridge is easy, no matter which mode of transportation you choose.

By Train

It takes less than an hour to get to Cambridge from London by train, making this the top method. The Greater Anglia, which departs from Liverpool Street, and the Great Northern operating out of King's Cross, will take you to Cambridge easily with their frequent services. The only thing that may add to your time is walking, as Cambridge's station is about 25 minutes from the main attractions.

By Coach Bus

A coach bus is a slower way to get to Cambridge, especially if you are journeying out that way during rush hour. However, coach buses are also an efficient way to save money. Coach buses depart regularly from the Victoria Coach Station to take you to Cambridge. Remember that if you intend to only be in Cambridge for the day, the bus can take up to two-and-a-half hours, impacting your plans for making it to your destination.

By Car

Car is the last option (and not the best option), as we've explored earlier, given the congestion charges and so on. Getting to Cambridge by car can also take longer if you hit some traffic. If you plan to drive to Cambridge, park at one of their city park-and-ride locations, where you can catch a bus to take you around the city.

What NOT to Do in Cambridge

Cambridge is a quaint, quintessential town that should be on your bucket list. Here are a couple of things to remember when you go!

Don't Forget to Visit the University Colleges

Yes, Cambridge has 31 universities and colleges in its town. When school is in session, the population of Cambridge seems to double or triple in size! Although there are a lot of colleges and universities to visit, these buildings are rich with history, and the architecture is beautiful, so don't forget to go and wander around to view them! (Also, remember not to interrupt a class.)

Don't Swim or Boat in the River Cam Without Permission

Swimming and boating in the River Cam without proper authorization can be dangerous and is often restricted.

Don't Miss Punting

It might seem like a cliché thing to do in Cambridge, but punting around the River Cam is a lot of fun. You can rent your own or be chauffeured, but either way, it's an enjoyable way to spend a couple of hours seeing the different sights of Cambridge.

Don't Ignore Quiet Hours

Many areas in Cambridge, especially residential neighborhoods, have quiet hours in the evenings. Be mindful of noise levels and respect local regulations.

It may be tempting to stay within London's city limits because, as you have read, there are many things to see and do. But taking a day trip or two outside of London is also worthwhile because you can immerse yourself in other ways of living away from the bustling city and see different things related to the Royal family and other mysterious landmarks like Stonehenge.

Planning a trip to London should be a fun thing to do. While there is plenty to see and do from City of London to West London and beyond England's capital, you have been given several things to consider when planning your trip (and things to avoid) to make your trip to London the trip of your life!

That's it! Congratulations, you have made it to the end of the book!

Conclusion

A s England's biggest capital city, London is a diverse city, rich with history, landmarks, and monuments throughout its many areas. I can understand if you feel overwhelmed and unsure of where to begin. The first step is to start planning. The second step is to use this book as your guide as it brings you through many famous attractions. The attractions and landmarks mentioned in this book will help you figure out what you must see and do in London.

Here's the thing to remember, though: You were given plenty of ideas on where to go and stay and what to experience. In reality, you won't see everything on the first trip (or even the second or third). But that's the fun part about traveling, especially if you have a travel bug. With the landmarks and things to do that I've provided, go back and make a list of the things that resonated with you in each of the areas of London and then narrow them down based on how long you'll be on your vacation.

As you travel through London, remember to keep the what *not* to do tips and tricks close at hand to ensure a memorable trip without stress or disappointment.

Armed with the knowledge and insights from this book, explore London with a sense of curiosity, wonder, and a commitment to embracing the magnetism that makes this global city truly special. Step into the vibrant embrace of London and let its magnetic charm transform you.

If this book has served you well in preparing for your trip, please give the gift of travel and leave a review on Amazon.

Glossary

- **A-Z:** A map guide of London.

- **Buck House:** Another way to refer to Buckingham Palace.

- **Congestion charge:** A central London tax is added on when cars enter the congestion charge zone.

- **GMT:** Greenwich Mean Time

- **M25:** An orbital highway circling London.

- **Mind the gap:** A warning to be careful of the gap between the tube car and the platform.

- **Tube:** London's subway system.

- **Zebra crossing:** A crosswalk for pedestrians.

British Slang

This section is a compilation of British slang you may hear.

- **Chips:** The name for thick-cut fries.
- **Innit:** A shorter way to ask, "Isn't it?" In other words, it's a way to say, "Don't you agree?"
- **Loo:** Another way to say "bathroom."
- **Mate:** Another way to say "friend."
- **Quid:** A quid is another way to say "pound," such as "That will be five quid."

The Travel Enthusiast's Guide to Cockney Slang

Weather

- **Currant bun:** The Sun or the Sun Newspaper.

- **David Starkey:** Parkey, as in being cold.

- **Mork and Mindy:** A way to say it's windy.

- **Peas in the pot:** Sometimes shortened to peas or peasy, this phrase means that it is hot.

- **Taters in the mold:** Often shortened to taters, it's another way to say it's cold.

- **Ache and pain:** Cockney slang to say it's raining.

Eating and Drinking

- **Fisherman's daughter:** A way to say "a glass of water."

- **Loop the loop:** A way to say "soup."

- **Rosy Lee:** A way to say "a cup of tea."

- **Rub-a-dub-dub or rub-a-dug:** A way to say "pub."

- **Vera Lynn:** A way to say "a shot of gin."

- **Chewy toffee:** A way to say "a cup of coffee."

- **Battlecruiser:** A way to call someone a "boozer."

- **Near and far:** A way to say a "bar."

- **Brahms and Liszt:** A way to say "pissed" (or very drunk).

References

About Camden Town. (n.d.). Camden Town. https://camdentown.info/discover/about-camden-town

About the forest. (n.d.). Epping Forest Heritage Trust. https://efht.org.uk/discover-epping-forest/about-the-forest/

Access, facilities, and FAQ. (n.d.). Westminster Abbey. https://www.westminster-abbey.org/visit-us/plan-your-visit/access-facilities-and-faq

All Saints Church, Kingston upon Thames. (n.d.). What's on in Kingston upon Thames? https://www.whatsoninkingstonuponthames.com/all-saints-church-kingston-upon-thames/

Allen, A. (2022, October 25). *The best streets in Shoreditch, London, to see graffiti.* Culture Trip. https://theculturetrip.com/europe/united-kingdom/england/london/articles/shoreditch-s-best-street-art-east-london-graffiti-you-need-to-see/

Angel, D. (2023, February 14). *Sixteen old streets in London: London's oldest streets (+maps & local tips).* Delve into Europe. https://delveintoeurope.com/old-streets-in-london/

Around the Horniman. (n.d.). Horniman Museum and Gardens. https://www.horniman.ac.uk/plan-your-visit/around-the-horniman/

Balston, J. (2018, June 24). *The Vicar's Oak.* The Triangle SE19. https://thetriangle19.blogspot.com/2018/06/the-vicars-oak.html

Bank of England Museum. (n.d.). Visit London. https://www.visitlondon.com/things-to-do/place/611007-bank-of-england-museum

BAPS Shri Swaminarayan Mandir (Neasden Temple). (n.d.). Visit London. https://www.visitlondon.com/things-to-do/place/1123165-baps-shri-swaminarayan-mandir-neasden-temple

Barker, S. (2023, May 10). This multi-story car park hides a food & drink hotspot centered around the community. *Secret London.* https://secretldn.com/peckham-levels-food-art-culture/

Barnaby, J. (2020, May 12). *43 London quotes that say everything you need to know...* London X London. https://www.londonxlondon.com/london-quotes/#:~:text=%E2%80%9CBy%20seeing%20London%2C%20I%20have

Barnaby, J. (2022a, January 25). *Nineteen cool things to do in Brixton.* London X London. https://www.londonxlondon.com/things-to-do-in-brixton/

Barnaby, J. (2022b, February 25). *Nunhead Cemetery – visiting South London's gothic gem.* London X London. https://www.londonxlondon.com/nunhead-cemetery/

Barnaby, J. (2022c, May 13). *Best things to do in Greenwich, London.* London X London. https://www.londonxlondon.com/things-to-do-in-greenwich/

Barnaby, J. (2023a, March 6). *The ultimate Shoreditch street art guide: 18 unmissable spots + map.* London X London. https://www.londonxlondon.com/street-art-in-shoreditch-free-tour/

Barnaby, J. (2023b, May 26). *Time to discover: London's Little Venice.* London X London. https://www.londonxlondon.com/little-venice-london/

Barnaby, J. (2023c, June 22). *London travel trips: 45 ridiculously useful tips for traveling to London (written by a local).* London X London. https://www.londonxlondon.com/best-london-travel-tips/

Barnaby, J. (2023d, June 22). *The best things to do in Notting Hill, London.* London X London. https://www.londonxlondon.com/things-to-do-in-notting-hill/

Barnaby, J. (2023e, July 24). *Twenty-three beautiful parks in South London you should explore.* London X London. https://www.londonxlondon.com/best-parks-in-south-london/

Barratt, B. (2022, June 11). *The best hotels in West London.* Culture Trip. https://theculturetrip.com/europe/united-kingdom/england/london/articles/the-best-hotels-in-west-london

Beard, G. (2019a, June 28). *Nine things that tourists should never do in London.* Culture Trip. https://theculturetrip.com/europe/united-kingdom/england/london/articles/10-things-you-should-never-ever-do-in-london/

Beard, G. (2019b, November 29). *A guide to Peckham, South London.* Culture Trip. https://theculturetrip.com/europe/united-kingdom/england/london/articles/a-guide-to-peckham-south-london/

Bertazzo, S. (2016, April 12). *Fourteen things to never do in London.* The Spotahome Blog. https://www.spotahome.com/blog/14-things-to-never-do-in-london/

Best 15 Thames river boat trips and tours. (n.d.). Visit London. https://www.visitlondon.com/things-to-do/sightseeing/sightseeing-tours/river-tour

Best 25 things to do in Camden Town. (n.d.). Visit London. https://www.visitlondon.com/things-to-do/london-areas/camden-town/things-to-do-camden-town

Best London tour packages. (n.d.). Visit London. https://www.visitlondon.com/things-to-do/sightseeing/sightseeing-tours/london-tour-packages

Best places to stay in East London. (2023, February 21). BEAST London. https://beastmag.co.uk/places-to-stay/best-places-to-stay-in-east-london/

Bianca. (2020, April 21). *Kensington area guide.* London Kensington Guide. https://www.londonkensingtonguide.com/kensington/

Bianca. (2022, December 21). *Eleven best markets in North London.* London Kensington Guide. https://www.londonkensingtonguide.com/markets-in-north-london/

Bianca. (2023, March 12). *Twenty cool things to do in Paddington.* London Kensington Guide. https://www.londonkensingtonguide.com/things-to-do-in-paddington/

Biancolin, B. (2018, August 29). *Ten annoying things tourists do in London (11 tips to blend in like a local).* TheTravel. https://www.thetravel.com/10-annoying-things-tourists-do-in-london-11-tips-to-blend-in-like-a-local

Billingsgate Roman House and Baths. (n.d.). City of London. https://www.thecityoflondon.com/directory/billingsgate-roman-house-and-baths/

Bird, A. (2023a, May 1). *Fifteen best things to do in Croydon* https://www.thecrazytourist.com/15-best-things-to-do-in-croydon-london-boroughs-england/. The Crazy Tourist. https://www.thecrazytourist.com/15-best-things-to-do-in-croydon-london-boroughs-england/

Bird, A. (2023b, May 1). *Fifteen best things to do in Hammersmith (London boroughs, England).* The Crazy Tourist. https://www.thecrazytourist.com/15-best-things-to-do-in-hammersmith-london-boroughs-england/

Book sightseeing tickets. (n.d.). St Paul's Cathedral. https://www.stpauls.co.uk/book-tickets

Bridgerton. (2020). Netflix.

Britannica, T. Editors of Encyclopaedia. (2019). Croydon. In *Encyclopædia Britannica.* https://www.britannica.com/place/Croydon-borough-London

British culture and social norms. (n.d.). Study in the UK. https://www.studying-in-uk.org/british-culture-and-social-norms/

British etiquette and culture. (2023, June 27). Expatica. https://greatbritishmag.co.uk/uk-culture/top-ten-british-etiquette-tips/

Brobbey, S. (n.d.). *5 of the best things to do in Brixton.* Visit London. https://www.visitlondon.com/things-to-do/london-areas/brixton/reasons-to-visit-brixton

Burback, E. (2022, November 8). *A brief history of Windsor Castle.* Town & Country. https://www.townandcountrymag.com/society/tradition/a40058863/windsor-castle-history/

Byrne, C. (2023, January 2). *The best hotels to book in East London.* Culture Trip. https://theculturetrip.com/europe/united-kingdom/england/london/articles/the-best-hotels-in-east-london/

Carroll, R. (2022, October 25). *What's the difference between London and the City of London?* Culture Trip. https://theculturetrip.com/europe/united-kingdom/england/london/articles/whats-the-difference-between-london-and-the-city-of-london/

Caster, Y. (2023, February 28). *Windsor travel guide.* Times Travel. https://www.thetimes.co.uk/travel/destinations/uk/england/windsor/

Changing the Guard at Buckingham Palace. (n.d.). Visit London. https://www.visitlondon.com/things-to-do/event/8725947-changing-the-guard

Christina. (2023, February 20). *Visit London like a smartie: 18 London travel mistakes to avoid.* Happy to Wander. https://happytowander.com/visit-london-like-a-smartie-london-travel-mistakes-to-avoid/

City Visitor Trail. (n.d.). Visit London. https://www.visitlondon.com/things-to-do/place/30101525-city-visitor-trail

Cogan, J. (2021, August 3). *Top things to see and do in Fulham, London*. Culture Trip. https://theculturetrip.com/europe/united-kingdom/england/london/articles/top-10-things-to-see-and-do-in-fulham

Columbia Road Flower Market. (n.d.). Visit London. https://www.visitlondon.com/things-to-do/place/285623-columbia-road-flower-market

Columbus, C. (Director). (2001). *Harry Potter and the philosopher's stone* [Film]. Warner Bros. Pictures.

Columbus, C. (Director). (2002). *Harry Potter and the chamber of secrets* [Film]. Warner Bros. Pictures.

David. (2019a, February 28). *Things to know about Holland Parks' Kyoto Garden*. Park Grand. https://www.parkgrandkensington.co.uk/blog/things-to-know-about-kyoto-garden/

David. (2019b, March 25). *Which museums should you visit on Museum Mile if time is of the essence?* Park Grand. https://www.parkgrandkensington.co.uk/blog/museums-visit-museum-mile-time-essence/

David. (2020, February 24). *A definitive guide to London's West End*. The Piccadilly London West End. https://www.thepiccadillywestend.co.uk/blog/a-definitive-guide-to-londons-west-end/

Dearsley, B. (2022, January 31). *From London to Windsor Castle: 5 best ways to get there*. Planetware. https://www.planetware.com/england/from-london-to-windsor-castle-best-ways-to-get-there-eng-1-36.htm

Dearsley, B. (2023, May 11). *From London to Cambridge: 3 best ways to get there*. Planetware. https://www.planetware.com/england/from-london-to-cambridge-best-ways-to-get-there-eng-1-57.htm

Dekel-Daks, T. (2023, July 4). *How does the Wimbledon 2023 queue work?* House & Garden. https://www.houseandgarden.co.uk/article/wimbledon-2023-queue-tips

Dellow, J. (2022, June 28). *Cool hotels in West London to book a room in*. Love and London. https://loveandlondon.com/cool-hotels-in-west-london-to-book-a-room-in/

Docklands Light Railway (DLR). (n.d.). Visit London. https://www.visitlondon.com/traveller-information/getting-around-london/docklands-light-railway-network

Dodgson, L. (2019, January 19). *11 etiquette rules you need to know before visiting the UK*. Insider. https://www.insider.com/british-etiquette-rules-to-know-before-visiting-uk-2019-1

Donna-Kay. (2022, July 5). *Where to stay in East London: hotels and best areas*. Hues of Delahaye. https://www.huesofdelahaye.com/where-stay-east-london/

Donna-Kay. (2023, July 22). *Twenty-four best things to do in Westminster London (2023)*. Hues of Delahaye. https://www.huesofdelahaye.com/things-to-do-in-westminster-london/

Durante, I. (2022, October 14). *Tourist scams in London*. INSIDE. https://insidr.co/tourist-scams-in-london

Editor. (2023, April 10). *Tips when visiting historical sites*. MrPassenger. https://mrpassenger.com/tips-when-visiting-historical-sites/

Eighteen things to do in Stratford. (n.d.). Thingstodoinlondon.com. https://www.thingstodoinlondon.com/where/stratford/

11 mistakes people make when visiting London. (n.d.). Hotels.com. https://ph.hotels.com/go/england/mistakes-people-make-when-visiting-london

11 Things to do in Hammersmith. (n.d.). Thingstodoinlondon.com. https://www.thingstodoinlondon.com/where/hammersmith/

English Heritage: Eltham Palace. (n.d.). Visit London. https://www.visitlondon.com/things-to-do/place/344334-english-heritage-eltham-palace

Experience the Ceremony of the Keys. (n.d.). Tower of London. https://www.hrp.org.uk/tower-of-london/whats-on/ceremony-of-the-keys/

Explore Kingston upon Thames and places to visit in Kingston upon Thames. (n.d.). What's on in Kingston upon Thames. https://www.whatsoninkingstonuponthames.com/attractions-places-to-visit/

Family day out on South Bank and Bankside. (n.d.). Visit London. https://www.visitlondon.com/things-to-do/sightseeing/one-day-itineraries/family-day-out-on-south-bank-and-bankside

15 best markets in East London guide (2023). (n.d.). CK Travels. https://www.cktravels.com/best-markets-east-london/

15 things to do in and around Earl's Court. (n.d.). Apple & Pie Blackbird. https://www.blackbirdearlscourt.co.uk/things-to-do-in-earls-court

Forge, K. (2023, May 9). *10 terrific things to do in Tooting that are toot-ally brilliant*. Secret London. https://secretldn.com/things-to-do-in-tooting/

Forty Hall's families and history. (n.d.). Forty Hall Estate. https://www.fortyhallestate.co.uk/page/history/

Franchesca. (2019, March 27). *What not to do in London, England*. Trip101. https://trip101.com/article/what-not-to-do-in-london

Frohlich, L. (2017, July 2). *7 simple reasons why you need to visit Chiswick*. Secret London. https://secretldn.com/7-simple-reasons-need-visit-chiswick/

Girl Gone London. (2022, October 1). *9+ attractions you must book ahead of time in London (2023)*. https://girlgonelondon.com/attractions-to-book-ahead-of-time-in-london/

Guildhall Art Gallery. (n.d.). Guildhall. https://www.guildhall.cityoflondon.gov.uk/spaces/guildhall-art-gallery

Guildhall Art Gallery & Roman Amphitheatre. (n.d.). Visit London. https://www.visitlondon.com/things-to-do/place/157999-guildhall-art-gallery-and-roman-amphitheatre

Gunn, Z. (2023, July 17). *The best restaurants in the City of London*. Luxury London. https://luxurylondon.co.uk/taste/food/best-restaurants-in-the-city-of-london-liverpool-street-st-pauls-square-mile/

Hampton Court Palace. (n.d.). What's on in Kingston upon Thames. https://www.whatsoninkingstonuponthames.com/hampton-court-palace/

Highgate Cemetery. (n.d.). Visit London. https://www.visitlondon.com/things-to-do/place/149369-highgate-cemetery

History. (n.d.). Www.stonehenge.co.uk. https://www.stonehenge.co.uk/stonehenge

History of Guildhall Art Gallery. (2022, June 27). City of London. https://www.cityoflondon.gov.uk/things-to-do/attractions-museums-entertainment/guildhall-art-gallery/about/history

How to blend in with the locals in London. (2023, March 5). Stayo. https://stayo.com/journal/how-to-blend-in-with-the-locals-in-london/

How to get from London to Stonehenge (tour, train, bus, car). (n.d.). UK Travel Planning.com. https://uktravelplanning.com/london-to-stonehenge/

How to save money in London. (n.d.). Visit London. https://www.visitlondon.com/things-to-do/budget-london/top-11-moneysaving-tips-for-visiting-london

IFS Cloud Cable Car. (n.d.). Visit London. https://www.visitlondon.com/things-to-do/tickets/25549367-london-cable-car

Jack The Ripper Walking Tour. (n.d.). Visit London. https://www.visitlondon.com/things-to-do/place/49022960-jack-the-ripper-walking-tour

Jackie. (2011, January 30). *London Hotels: Top Tips For Booking Your Hotel Room – Guide to London Hotel Realities*. Londontopia. https://londontopia.net/guides/london-hotels-top-tips-for-booking-your-hotel-room-london-hotel-realities/

Johnson, B. (n.d.). *London's Roman Amphitheatre*. Historic UK. https://www.historic-uk.com/HistoryMagazine/DestinationsUK/Londons-Roman-Amphitheatre/

Jonathan. (2012, January 24). *London lingo: a London word dictionary – words unique to London*. Londontopia. https://londontopia.net/site-news/featured/london-lingo-a-london-word-dictionary-words-unique-to-london/

Jurga. (2023a, January 20). *What to do in Greenwich: 23 top places (+map & one day intinerary)*. Full Suitcase Family Travel Blog. https://fullsuitcase.com/things-to-do-in-greenwich/

Jurga. (2023b, May 16). *Where to stay in London (2023): 7 best areas, map & hotels for all budgets*. Full Suitcase. https://fullsuitcase.com/london-where-to-stay/

Justine. (2022, April 23). *9 surprisingly helpful tips on things to avoid in London*. Journeying the Globe. https://jtgtravel.com/europe/united-kingdom/things-to-avoid-in-london

Karen. (n.d.). *Mistakes to avoid in London, England*. Forever Karen. https://foreverkaren.com/travel/mistakes-to-avoid-in-london/

Kendrick, L. (2022, July 15). *The best things to do in Fulham*. London X London. https://www.londonxlondon.com/things-to-do-fulham/

Kennedy, M. (2012, June 5). *Shakespeare's Curtain theatre unearthed in East London*. *The Guardian*. https://www.theguardian.com/culture/2012/jun/06/shakespeare-curtain-theatre-shoreditch-east-lonfon

Kensington Palace, London. (n.d.). London Toolkit. https://www.londontoolkit.com/whattodo/kensington_palace.htm

Kepnes, M. (2023, July 21). *Where to Stay in London (Updated 2023)*. Nomadic Matt. https://www.nomadicmatt.com/travel-blogs/where-to-stay-london

Kingston upon Thames. (n.d.). Visit Surrey. https://www.visitsurrey.com/explore/kingston-upon-thames-p1232011

Know before you go: a traveler's guide to UK currency. (n.d.). TripSavvy. https://www.tripsavvy.com/basic-information-about-uk-currency-1582421

Lady's 5 things to do in Stoke Newington, London. (n.d.). A Lady in London. https://www.aladyinlondon.com/2021/06/things-to-do-stoke-newington.html

Lady's 15 North London neighbourhoods you'll love. (n.d.). A Lady in London. https://www.aladyinlondon.com/2021/05/north-london-neighborhoods.html

Lady's guide to things to do in Wapping, London. (n.d.). A Lady in London. https://www.aladyinlondon.com/2014/03/wapping-london-pubs-restaurants-sightseeing.html

Laliberte, M. (2022, March 16). *7 British etiquette rules Americans need to adopt*. Reader's Digest. https://www.rd.com/list/british-etiquette/

Lambeth Palace: the little known tour of a historic building. (n.d.). Slow Travel. https://www.slow-travel.uk/post/lambeth-palace

Landon, A. (2022, April 21). *10 of the very best things to do in Walthamstow*. Secret London. https://secretldn.com/10-reasons-walthamstow-area-guide/

Leadenhall Market. (n.d.). Visit London. https://www.visitlondon.com/things-to-do/place/1032022-leadenhall-market

Lee Valley and the Olympic Park, Stratford. (n.d.). Visit London. https://www.visitlondon.com/things-to-do/london-areas/lee-valley

Liu, A. (2023, March 10). *FAQ – things you can do or not do in Epping Forest*. Epping Forest Heritage Trust. https://efht.org.uk/faq-things-you-can-do-or-not-do-in-epping-forest/

Lloyd. (2023a, July 14). *13 very best things to do in Central London*. Hand Luggage Only. https://handluggageonly.co.uk/2022/09/08/13-very-best-things-to-do-in-central-london/

Lloyd. (2023b, July 14). *14 best things to do in North London*. Hand Luggage Only. https://handluggageonly.co.uk/2021/02/20/14-best-things-to-do-in-north-london/

Lloyd. (2023c, July 15). *9 best things to do in Whitechapel – London*. Hand Luggage Only. https://handluggageonly.co.uk/2016/04/08/a-locals-guide-9-of-the-best-places-to-discover-in-whitechapel-london/

Lloyd. (2023d, August 2). *16 best things to do in Cambridge, England*. Hand Luggage Only. https://handluggageonly.co.uk/2018/01/12/16-best-things-cambridge-england/

Local trains in London. (n.d.). Visit London. https://www.visitlondon.com/traveller-information/getting-around-london/local-trains-in-london

London buses. (n.d.). Visit London. https://www.visitlondon.com/traveller-information/getting-around-london/london-bus

London cycle hire scheme. (n.d.). Visit London. https://www.visitlondon.com/traveller-information/getting-around-london/london-cycle-hire-scheme

London river bus services on the Thames. (n.d.). Visit London. https://www.visitlondon.com/traveller-information/getting-around-london/riverboat

London taxis, black cabs and minicabs. (n.d.). Visit London. https://www.visitlondon.com/traveller-information/getting-around-london/london-taxis

London trams. (n.d.). Visit London. https://www.visitlondon.com/traveller-information/getting-around-london/tram

London Underground. (n.d.). Visit London. https://www.visitlondon.com/traveller-information/getting-around-london/london-tube

London weather forecast. (n.d.). Visit London. https://www.visitlondon.com/weather

London X London. (2023, March 26). *Time to explore: King's Road, Chelsea*. https://www.londonxlondon.com/kings-road-chelsea/

London x London. (2022, June 16). *Best Things to do in South London: an insider's area guide*. https://www.londonxlondon.com/things-to-do-south-london/

London's Roman Amphitheatre. (n.d.-a). Britain Express. https://www.britainexpress.com/London/roman-amphitheatre.htm

London's Roman Amphitheatre. (n.d.-b). City of London. https://www.thecityofldn.com/directory/londons-roman-amphitheatre/

Louise, E. (2019, August 23). *London: Sundays at Victoria Park Market*. The Little Edition. https://little-edition.com/2019/08/22/london-sundays-at-victoria-park-market/

Lynch, L. (2021, December 17). *Things to do in Windsor: a perfect day trip from London*. Savored Journeys. https://www.savoredjourneys.com/day-trip-from-london-things-to-do-in-windsor/#8_Great_Things_to_Do_in_Windsor

Madame Tussauds London. (n.d.). Visit London. https://www.visitlondon.com/things-to-do/place/284875-madame-tussauds-london

Mind your manners – great British dining etiquette. (2023, February 22). Victoria Eggs. https://www.victoriaeggs.com/blogs/news/mind-your-manners-great-british-dining-etiquette

Museums and galleries. (n.d.). Visit Greenwich. https://www.visitgreenwich.org.uk/things-to-do/attractions/museums-and-galleries

Museums in London? Visit the exciting museum mile! (2019, July 20). Museum Spotlight Europe. https://museumspotlighteurope.com/need-an-exciting-museum-experience-try-londons-museum-mile/

Nick. (2017, May 20). *Using taxis and private hire car services in London*. My UK SIM Card. https://www.myuksimcard.com/blog/quick-guide-to-taxis-hire-cars-and-uber-in-london/

19 things to do in Wimbledon. (n.d.). Thingstodoinlondon.com. https://www.thingstodoinlondon.com/where/wimbledon/

Nix, E. (2023, May 16). *7 things you should know about Stonehenge*. History. https://www.history.com/news/7-things-you-should-know-about-stonehenge

Norah, L. (2023a, February 25). *London packing list: what to pack for London and the UK at any time of year*. Finding the Universe. https://www.findingtheuniverse.com/london-packing-list-what-to-pack-for-london-and-the-uk-at-any-time-of-year/

Norah, L. (2023b, April 26). *Where to stay in London: complete neighbourhood & accommodation guide*. Finding the Universe. https://www.findingtheuniverse.com/where-to-stay-london-accommodation-guide

Noyen, M. (2022, June 24). *I live in Notting Hill, London. Here are 5 things I wish tourists knew before visiting*. Insider. https://www.insider.com/notting-hill-london-what-to-know-about-visiting-by-local-2022-6

Nunhead Cemetery. (n.d.). Southwark Council. https://www.southwark.gov.uk/parks-and-open-spaces/parks/nunhead-cemetery

Oakley, M. (n.d.). *Wapping in East London: a historic riverside district with plenty to offer*. East London History. https://www.eastlondonhistory.co.uk/visit-wapping-east-london/

Oakley, M. (2014, February 28). *Stratford: a guide to East London's cultural hub*. East London History. https://www.eastlondonhistory.co.uk/visit-stratford-east-london/

Official London Eye tickets & prices. (n.d.). Lastminute.com London Eye. https://www.londoneye.com/tickets-and-prices/

150 years of Ally Pally. (n.d.). Alexandra Palace. https://www.alexandrapalace.com/150-campaign/150-overview/

Opening and closing times. (n.d.-a). Tower of London. https://www.hrp.org.uk/tower-of-london/visit/opening-and-closing-times/#gs.2tyck7

Opening and closing times. (n.d.-b). Kew. https://www.kew.org/kew-gardens/visit-kew-gardens/opening-and-closing-times

Our history. (n.d.). Horniman Museum and Gardens. https://www.horniman.ac.uk/our-history/

Our role in London. (2023, April 17). City of London. https://www.cityoflondon.gov.uk/about-us/about-the-city-of-london-corporation/our-role-in-london

Owens, J. (n.d.). *Stonehenge*. National Geographic. https://www.nationalgeographic.com/history/article/stonehenge-1

Parsons, G. (2023, February 20). *The incredibly ornate temple that you won't believe is in London – BAPS Shri Swaminarayan Mandir*. Secret London. https://secretldn.com/neasden-temple-hindu-london-mandir/

Pearson, M. (n.d.). *The best secret bars in East London*. The London Pass®. https://londonpass.com/en-us/blog/the-best-secret-bars-in-east-london

Places to visit in Cambridge. (n.d.). VisitEngland. https://www.visitengland.com/things-to-do/cambridge

Plan your visit to the Museum of London Docklands. (n.d.). Museum of London. https://www.museumoflondon.org.uk/museum-london-docklands/plan-your-visit

Porter, L. (2019, June 10). *Advice from Londoners: things not to do in London*. TripSavvy. https://www.tripsavvy.com/things-not-to-do-in-london-1583397

Portobello Market. (n.d.). Portobello Road. https://www.portobelloroad.co.uk/the-market/

Prices and opening times for Stonehenge. (n.d.). English Heritage. https://www.english-heritage.org.uk/visit/places/stonehenge/prices-and-opening-times/

Primrose Hill. (n.d.). The Royal Parks. https://www.royalparks.org.uk/parks/the-regents-park/things-to-see-and-do/primrose-hill

Rabon, J. (2018, May 30). *Top 10 London: top ten things to see and do in the Earl's Court area.* Londontopia. https://londontopia.net/guides/top-10-london-top-ten-things-see-earls-court-area/

Rabon, J. (2019, December 16). *London 101: where to go if you need help in London.* Londontopia. https://londontopia.net/travel/london-101-where-to-go-if-you-need-help-in-london/

Rachel. (2018, March 14). *How to save money on flights to London.* Days to Come. https://www.tourradar.com/days-to-come/how-to-save-money-on-flights-to-london/

Red Rooster. (2022, October 10). *15 things to do & places to visit in Canary Wharf.* Red Rooster London. https://redroosterldn.com/things-to-do-in-canary-wharf/

Reford, L. (2023, May 30). *Cockney rhyming slang 101: words and phrases to make you sound like the real deal.* London X London. https://www.londonxlondon.com/cockney-rhyming-slang/

Richmond Park. (n.d.-a). Visit London. https://www.visitlondon.com/things-to-do/place/62295-richmond-park

Richmond Park. (n.d.-b). The Royal Parks. https://www.royalparks.org.uk/parks/richmond-park

Royal Albert Hall tours. (n.d.). Royal Albert Hall. https://www.royalalberthall.com/plan-your-visit-essential-safety-information/tours/

Royal Botanic Gardens, Kew (Kew Gardens). (n.d.). Visit London. https://www.visitlondon.com/things-to-do/place/58711-royal-botanic-gardens-kew

Sadler, R. (2022a, July 12). *Best things to do in Stoke Newington.* London X London. https://www.londonxlondon.com/stoke-newington/

Sadler, R. (2022b, September 14). *Brilliant things to do in Walthamstow.* London X London. https://www.londonxlondon.com/things-to-do-walthamstow/

Security information. (n.d.). UK Parliament. https://www.parliament.uk/visiting/access/security/

Serrant, A. (2018, October 26). *The languages of London.* Museum of London. https://www.museumoflondon.org.uk/discover/languages-london

6 things you never knew about East London. (2017, November 17). Craft Gin Club. https://www.craftginclub.co.uk/ginnedmagazine/2017/11/17/6-things-you-never-knew-about-east-london

16 things to do in Wapping, London – by a local (2023). (n.d.). CK Travels. https://www.cktravels.com/things-to-do-in-wapping-london/

Sky Garden. (n.d.). Visit London. https://www.visitlondon.com/things-to-do/place/45317801-sky-garden

Sky Garden help center. (n.d.). Sky Garden. https://skygarden.london/faqs-search/

South Bank. (n.d.). Visit London. https://www.visitlondon.com/things-to-do/place/5207784-south-bank

Spencer, L. J. (2015, March 12). *The ruins of St. Dunstan-in-the-East.* Atlas Obscura. https://www.atlasobscura.com/places/the-ruins-of-st-dunstan-in-the-east

Statista Research Department. (2023, June 5). *Leading UK cities for international tourism 2019-2022, by visits.* Statista. https://www.statista.com/statistics/289010/top-50-uk-tourism-destinations/

St Dunstan in the East Church Garden. (n.d.). City of London. https://www.cityoflondon.gov.uk/things-to-do/city-gardens/find-a-garden/st-dunstan-in-the-east-church-garden

Steinbeck, J. (2017). *Travels with Charley : in search of America.* Penguin Books.

Syeda, A. (2023, March 30). *Best time To visit London - a month on month guide to visiting London.* Headout Blog. https://www.headout.com/blog/best-time-to-visit-london/

10 common mistakes tourists make when visiting London. (n.d.). LondonHut. https://www.londonhut.com/p/mistakes-tourists-make-in-london

10 things to do in Fulham. (n.d.). Thingstodoinlondon.com. https://www.thingstodoinlondon.com/where/fulham/

The best scenic spots to enjoy a picnic In West London. (2023, August 3). Nestor. https://www.nestorstay.com/blog/the-best-scenic-spots-to-enjoy-a-picnic-in-west-london/

The best things to do in North London: an insider's guide. (n.d.). London X London. https://www.londonxlondon.com/london-area-guides/north-london/

The Design Museum. (n.d.). Visit London. https://www.visitlondon.com/things-to-do/place/606805-design-museum

The history of Tower Bridge. (n.d.). Tower Bridge. https://www.towerbridge.org.uk/discover/history

The Lord Mayor's show. (n.d.). The Lord Mayor's Show. https://lordmayorsshow.london/

The Regent's Park with Primrose Hill. (n.d.). Visit London. https://www.visitlondon.com/things-to-do/place/607119-regents-park-and-primrose-hill

The Rookery, Streatham. (n.d.). Lambeth. https://www.lambeth.gov.uk/parks/rookery-streatham

The Stay Club. (2023, January 10). *A guide to stay safe in London.* https://www.thestayclub.com/blog/a-guide-to-stay-safe-in-london/

The ultimate guide to visiting Shoreditch. (n.d.). Strawberry Tours. https://strawberrytours.com/london-neighbourhoods-shoreditch

The ultimate guide to visiting the Twickenham Stadium. (n.d.). Strawberry Tours. https://strawberrytours.com/twickenham-stadium

The Vicar's Oak – where four boundaries meet. (2018, April 11). Crystal Palace Park. https://www.crystalpalaceparktrust.org/news/the-vicars-oak-where-four-boundaries-meet/

Things to do in King's Cross and St Pancras, London. (n.d.). Visit London. https://www.visitlondon.com/things-to-do/london-areas/kings-cross

Things to do in London Paddington. (n.d.). Visit London. https://www.visitlondon.com/things-to-do/london-areas/paddington/things-to-do-paddington

Things to do in Regent's Park London. (n.d.). Free Tours by Foot. https://freetoursbyfoot.com/regents-park-london/

Things to do in South Kensington. (n.d.). Visit London. https://www.visitlondon.com/things-to-do/london-areas/kensington-and-south-kensington/things-to-do-south-kensington

Things to do in the City. (n.d.). Visit London. https://www.visitlondon.com/things-to-do/london-areas/city-of-london/things-to-do-in-the-city-of-london

Things to do in Tooting. (n.d.). The Bare Traveller. https://www.thebaretraveller.com/england/visit-tooting

This tranquil Japanese garden is the perfect place for stressed out Londoners – Kyoto Garden at Holland Park. (2023, July 12). Secret London. https://secretldn.com/kyoto-garden-tranquil-japanese-london/

Thomson, L. (2022, August 24). *Places you should avoid on any trip to London.* Culture Trip. https://theculturetrip.com/europe/united-kingdom/england/london/articles/11-places-you-should-avoid-on-any-trip-to-london/

Ticket Information. (n.d.). Horniman Museum and Gardens. https://www.horniman.ac.uk/plan-your-visit/ticket-information/

Tickets and prices. (n.d.). Kew. https://www.kew.org/kew-gardens/visit-kew-gardens/tickets

Tikkanen, A. (2023). speakeasy. In *Encyclopedia Britannica.* https://www.britannica.com/topic/speakeasy

Time Out editors, & Thomas, R. (2021, July 30). *The best hotels in South London.* Time out London. https://www.timeout.com/london/hotels/the-best-hotels-in-south-london

Tips for visiting the Harry Potter studio tour. (n.d.). Rhubarb and Wren. https://rhubarbandwren.co.uk/tips-for-visiting-the-warner-bros-harry-potter-studio-tour/

Top things to do in Greenwich. (n.d.). Visit London. https://www.visitlondon.com/things-to-do/london-areas/greenwich/top-things-to-do-in-greenwich

Top tips for visiting Windsor Castle. (2019, March 27). Sir Christopher Wren. https://sirchristopherwren.co.uk/top-tips-for-visiting-windsor-castle/

Tours, G. (n.d.). *13 things not to do when visiting London.* Golden Tours. https://www.goldentours.com/travelblog/things-not-to-do-in-london

Tower of London. (n.d.). Visit London. https://www.visitlondon.com/things-to-do/place/22249-hm-tower-of-london

Travel From USA to UK - complete guide. (2022, December 6). Visit Visa Guide. https://visitvisaguide.com/uk-visa/travel-from-usa-to-uk-complete-guide

Trilivas, N. (2019, May 20). *Everything you need to know to drive in London.* TripSavvy. https://www.tripsavvy.com/driving-in-london-what-you-need-to-know-4582947

12 Things to do in Kensington. (n.d.). Thingstodoinlondon.com. https://www.thingstodoinlondon.com/where/kensington/

20 facts about London's culture. (n.d.). Greater London Authority. https://www.london.gov.uk/programmes-strategies/arts-and-culture/vision-and-strategy/20-facts-about-london%E2%80%99s-culture

23 things to do in Notting Hill, London - by a local (2023). (n.d.). CK Travels. https://www.cktravels.com/things-to-do-in-notting-hill-london/#1_Portobello_Road_Market

23 things to do in South Bank. (n.d.). Thingstodoinlondon.com. https://www.thingstodoinlondon.com/where/south-bank/

Twickenham Stadium tour and museum. (n.d.). Twickenham. https://worldrugbymuseum.com/book

Vhatia, A. (2023, February 7). *13 mistakes tourists should avoid in London.* The Travel. https://www.thetravel.com/mistakes-tourists-should-avoid-in-london/

Visit Buckingham Palace. (n.d.). Royal Collection Trust. https://www.rct.uk/visit/buckingham-palace

Visit Us. (n.d.). Freud Museum London. https://www.freud.org.uk/visit/

Voogt, C. (2021, June 16). *Essential things to do in Cambridge.* Plum Guide. https://www.plumguide.com/journal/things-to-do-in-cambridge

Warren, J. (2023, April 19). Museum of Shakespeare to open in London next year. *BBC News.* https://www.bbc.com/news/uk-england-london-65324686

Welcome to Tower Bridge. (n.d.). Tower Bridge. https://www.towerbridge.org.uk/your-visit/visitor-information

Welcome to up at the 02. (n.d.). The O2. https://www.theo2.co.uk/up-at-the-o2/climb

Wembley Stadium. (n.d.). Visit London. https://www.visitlondon.com/things-to-do/place/280244-wembley-stadium

West London. (n.d.). Kinleigh Folkard & Hayward. https://www.kfh.co.uk/west-london/

Westminster guide. (n.d.). Visit London. https://www.visitlondon.com/things-to-do/london-areas/westminster

Where to stay in South London: the 8 best neighborhoods (& 5 to skip!). (2023, May 25). London on My Mind. https://londonmymind.com/where-stay-south-london/

Whittingslow, J. (n.d.). *Know before you go: BAPS MANDIR.* Explore Gwinnett. https://www.exploregwinnett.org/the-latest/know-before-you-go-baps-mandir

Who built Windsor Castle? (n.d.). Royal Collection Trust. https://www.rct.uk/visit/windsor-castle/who-built-windsor-castle

Why London is actually a city within a city. (n.d.). Britain Explained. https://britainexplained.com/what-is-the-city-of-london/

Wilmot, E. (n.d.). *5 reasons to visit Richmond.* Visit London. https://www.visitlondon.com/things-to-do/london-areas/richmond/reasons-to-visit-richmond

Wilson-Powell, G. (2017, March 16). *10 great things to do and see in Hoxton, London.* Culture Trip. https://theculturetrip.com/europe/united-kingdom/england/london/articles/10-great-things-to-do-and-see-in-hoxton-london/

Wilson-Powell, G. (2023, January 1). *The top things to do in Camden Town.* Culture Trip. https://theculturetrip.com/europe/united-kingdom/england/london/articles/the-top-10-things-to-do-and-see-in-camden/

Windsor Castle. (n.d.). Visit London. https://www.visitlondon.com/things-to-do/place/427214-windsor-castle

Windsor, A. (n.d.). *10 reasons to visit Stratford.* Visit London. https://www.visitlondon.com/things-to-do/london-areas/stratford/reasons-to-visit-stratford

Winterville Staff. (2022, June 16). *A travel guide to Notting Hill + things to do in Notting Hill.* Winterville. https://winterville.co.uk/notting-hill/#Shop_at_Portobello_Road_Market

Wolters World. (2019). Stonehenge - The don'ts of visiting Stonehenge. In *YouTube.* https://www.youtube.com/watch?v=yoGoMlUagQU

Zemler, E. (2020a, March 12). *The top 12 things to do in London's Chelsea neighborhood.* TripSavvy. https://www.tripsavvy.com/top-things-to-do-in-chelsea-london-4781144

Zemler, E. (2020b, July 10). *The Top 10 Things to Do in Whitechapel, London.* TripSavvy. https://www.tripsavvy.com/top-things-to-do-in-whitechapel-london-4788360

Zemler, E. (2022, October 12). *Where to stay in London: neighborhoods and hotels for every type of traveler.* Travel + Leisure. https://www.travelandleisure.com/hotels-resorts/where-to-stay-in-london#toc-where-to-stay-in-southbank

Image References

aitoff. (2016). Paddington Bear [Image]. In *Pixabay.* https://pixabay.com/photos/paddington-bear-station-statue-1708630/

Brierley, J. (2020). A shot of the back of St Pauls Cathedral London, UK [Image]. In *Unsplash.* https://unsplash.com/photos/cBTd4mUoJ5E

eduard. (2016). Gray concrete walls [Image]. In *Unsplash.* https://unsplash.com/photos/l29U993HB5A

Ehlers, S. (2018). Platform 9 3/4. In *Unsplash.* https://unsplash.com/photos/ltFKYpgoKto

Fewings, N. (2021). An old fashioned police box, used to call the police and famously used as the TARDIS in Doctor Who. [Image]. In *Unsplash.* https://unsplash.com/photos/AaVVJMwolic

hulkiokantabak. (2020). Speak no evil [Image]. In *pixabay.* https://pixabay.com/photos/shoreditch-london-uk-england-4897926/

Hurry, S. (2021). The long walk [Image]. In *Unsplash.* https://unsplash.com/photos/-gAJ2cfsCF4

Kuriyan, S. (2020). Stonehenge [Image]. In *Unsplash.* https://unsplash.com/photos/Xhax9gbaZzs

Letek, M. (2019). Exterior of Kew Gardens with fountain [Image]. In *Unsplash.* https://unsplash.com/photos/4dRCfIS25rw

LucieLucy. (2015). Changing of the Guards [Image]. In *Pixabay.* https://pixabay.com/photos/changing-of-the-guards-great-britain-959470/

McAllister, S. (2018). From Roger Federer's opening match in the 2018 Championships at Wimbledon against Dusan Lajovic of Serbia. [Image]. In *Unsplash.* https://unsplash.com/photos/J1j3cImjmgE

Medienservice. (2018). Nottinghill houses [Image]. In *Pixabay.* https://pixabay.com/photos/london-nottinghill-portobello-road-3628224/

Postiaux, C. (2018). Tower Bridge [Image]. In *Unsplash.* https://unsplash.com/photos/Q6UehpkBSnQ

Rauber, D. (2017). The entrance hall of the National History Museum in London is a breathtaking architectural artwork with a beautiful skeleton of a blue whale floating in the middle of the hall. It was my first trip to London when I took this photo. [Image]. In *Unsplash.* https://unsplash.com/photos/i2DUwXZDGAM

Rhii Photography. (2018). Person about to touch the hippogriff [Image]. In *Unslash.* https://unsplash.com/photos/nK1nJ3eA3eA

Seremet, D. (2021). Brown concrete building under cloudy sky during daytime [Image]. In *Unsplash.* https://unsplash.com/photos/5iU2A4fW6YA

Skitterphoto. (2017). Abbey Road [Image]. In *Pixabay.* https://pixabay.com/photos/abbey-road-crossing-zebra-europe-2293953/

Stöhr, F. (2019). Car parked near building [Image]. In *Unsplash.* https://unsplash.com/photos/Q6UehpkBSnQ

Van de Pol, A. (2017). Touring London [Image]. In *Unsplash.* https://unsplash.com/photos/tZDtyUrYrFU

Wheatley, T. (2019). Regent's Park pathway [Image]. In *Unsplash.* https://unsplash.com/photos/QcoS-WiyXtA

Made in United States
Troutdale, OR
04/23/2024

19399741R00086